HERCOLE BOTTRIGARI

IL DESIDERIO

AMERICAN INSTITUTE OF MUSICOLOGY
ARMEN CARAPETYAN, PH. D., DIRECTOR

MUSICOLOGICAL STUDIES AND DOCUMENTS

9

HERCOLE BOTTRIGARI

IL DESIDERIO

VINCENZO GIUSTINIANI

DISCORSO SOPRA LA MUSICA

MUSICOLOGICAL STUDIES AND DOCUMENTS

9

1. HERCOLE BOTTRIGARI

IL DESIDERIO

OR

CONCERNING THE PLAYING TOGETHER OF VARIOUS MUSICAL INSTRUMENTS

2. VICENZO GIUSTINIANI

DISCORSO SOPRA LA MUSICA

TRANSLATED BY

CAROL Mac CLINTOCK

AMERICAN INSTITUTE OF MUSICOLOGY

1962

IL DESIDERIO

OR

CONCERNING THE PLAYING TOGETHER OF VARIOUS MUSICAL INSTRUMENTS

DIALOGUE

BY THE

ILLUSTRIOUS SIGNORE CAVALIERE

M. HERCOLE BOTTRIGARI

IN WHICH ALSO IS DISCUSSED THE TUNING OF THESE
INSTRUMENTS, AND MANY OTHER THINGS
PERTINENT TO MUSIC

FOREWORD

Il Desiderio, the best known of Ercole Bottrigari's treatises on music, first published in 1594, has long been considered an important source of information about Sixteenth-century practice. Copies of it exist in many libraries, excerpts have appeared in sundry histories of music and elsewhere, but the volume had not been reprinted since 1601, until in 1924 Kathi Meyer brought out a facsimile of the second (1599) edition * with an important introduction describing Bottrigari's life, his works, and containing also a discussion of the publication and the various editions. Professor Gustave Reese in 1957, in his pamphlet *Fourscore Classics of Music Literature,* placed high on his list of desiderata the translation of *Il Desiderio* into English. Like Rabelais' priests, who were "deaf in their Latin ear", some students find that Seicento Italian, especially of the learned variety such as Bottrigari's, is pretty hard to understand. If this translation makes *Il Desiderio* more easily accessible to all scholars and more useful to English-speaking musicologists, it will serve the purpose for which it was undertaken.

Perhaps a word would be in season about some of the knotty problems with which the translator of Bottrigari is confronted. In the first place, the treatise is written in what D. P. Walker in *Die Musik in Geschichte und Gegenwart* calls "einen ausserordentlich schwer verständlichen Stil". The prose tradition of the Seicento was purely Ciceronian, with long complex sentences, concessive clauses, unmarked parentheses, and no or completely disorganized punctuation — all the apparatus of the Schoolmen. Even in the hands of a great literary artist this style is difficult and confusing; in the case of Bottrigari, no literary genius, it becomes atrocious. To make reading easier the translator has broken up many of the long, intricate, complex sentences into manageable pieces and has supplied modern punctuation. The huge slabs have been carved into bite-sized bits more digestible to Twentieth-century readers. There is no sacrifice of meaning; on the contrary, this practice greatly improves the clarity of the exposition, as a comparison of the English and the Italian versions will amply demonstrate.

In the second place, the technical terminology, often translated from the Latin or Greek, is confused and confusing, the interpretation being by no

* The present translation was made from this facsimile.

means certain. Especially is this true of the vocabulary which Bottrigari translates from Aristoxenus. The Italian writer is attempting to reconcile the basically mathematical harmonic theories of the ancients with the current practice of tempering of his own time; the inevitable result is a certain amount of confusion as to exact meaning of terms.

I am grateful to Professor Roy T. Will of Wayne State University and Professor Robert E. Mueller of Southern Illinois University for their help and advice in matters of Bottrigari's terminology. Thanks also are due to Professor Lander MacClintock, my husband, for his unfailing help with linguistic difficulties.

Note: Bottrigari's marginal headings are indicated by small letters in the footnotes. Only those headings which contain references or explain the matter under discussion are cited.

TO THE KIND AND COURTEOUS READER

So great, and so burning a desire to understand and learn the theoretical things of music entered the mind of M. Annibale Melone in his mature years that, in a way, he little prized those practical things of which, by having sung and played many kinds of musical instruments, and having composed Madrigals and Motets, and having taught others in the public school, he had made an honored and useful profession. In both his youth and in his prime he had been able not only to meet his needs but had made such an accumulation of Fortune's goods that in his old age he had no fear of poverty. He sought diligently and with all his powers to know, to speak with, and to frequent the society of any person who took pleasure in musical theory, and wished to be known himself as a theorist by them and by everyone. When it happened that having learned of the return in 1587 of the Cavaliere Ercole Bottrigari from Ferrara, where he had lived for many years, to his native city — knowing how much the Sig. Cavaliere had devoted himself to this particular study of Music along with other various studies of Mathematics; and how in his youth having composed very pleasing *Cantilene,* later, turning to speculation, he had taken delight in reading the works of the theorists, both ancient and modern, in Latin and Greek as well as in Italian — M. Melone devoted himself with every affection, diligence, and solicitude to acting as the worthy and faithful servitor of this other Gentleman. Bottrigari, having known of Melone for some time, received him with the greatest courtesy and with familiar intimacy and became his friend, so that out of the 24 hours of each day, at least 3 during the daytime in Summer and 3 in the evening in Winter Melone was in the house of the Cavaliere continually discussing with him matters pertinent to Music and to its theory.

All this, Kind Reader, I have wished to narrate in full, since you have seen this Dialogue about Concerts of various musical instruments, entitled IL DESIDERIO, issue from the press not many years ago under the false name of a supposed author. Do not marvel, then, that you see it here with the true name of its real author, that is, the aforesaid Sig. Cavaliere who, since he wrote the Dialogue at the instigation or stimulus of, and for the contemplation and satisfaction of Melone, introduced him into the discussion under the very apt name and surname of Alemanno Benelli. By means of an Anagram, or transposition of letters, this reveals none other than Annibale Melone. Likewise, Sig. Gratioso Desiderio is none other than that same M. Desiderio introduced by the learned Rev. Zarlino into his Dialogues, the *Dimostrationi armoniche.* An innate desire and feeling in the souls of men is to understand and to know about various things. And although it might seem to be a reply by Benelli to Gratioso when he said, "You wouldn't really belong in your family if you didn't DESIRE some fine thing at all times, and such is really your name," this was said very likely as a joke when the two were talking together. The present Dialogue was written, then, by the Sig. Cavaliere for the satisfaction, and at the instigation, of Melone, as also were written by him (Bottrigari) the *Three Dialogues of the Tones, Tropes, and Modes,* into which Melone was openly introduced as the principal speaker, and *Il Melone,* and *Il Melone Secondo,* where the three harmonic genera are discussed. For the contemplation of the same Melone Bottrigari likewise translated into the Italian language not only the *Harmonics* of Aristoxenus and of Ptolemy, purging them of the many errors found in a Latin translation of Gogavinus, and by brief annotations clearing up many obscurities, he also explained the Harmonic Rule of Euclid together with the *Isagoge,* or *Introduction,* with simple and brief demonstrations. In addition, he translated the 19th Division of the *Problems* of Aristotle, the *Sinopsis,* or *Compendio musicale* of Psellus, the *Musica* of Plutarch, that of Gaudentius, and that of Alipius. All these authors wrote in the Greek language, of which Melone did not understand a single word. And of the authors who wrote in Latin, in which Melone was entirely unsure of himself, several were likewise translated; the writings of Martianus Cappella, Censorino, Cassiodorus, Bede, some of the *Musica* of Fogliano, and also that of Boethius. It appeared to Melone that it was a fine opportunity to make himself universally known by publishing the *Dialogue.* He had already done this partially in some of his letters to Zarlino, to the Rev. Don Giovanni di Montoya *spagnuolo,* and other authors. Therefore he kept begging the Cavaliere to permit the *Dialogue* to be published, as also he begged him to permit the one and the other *Melone* to be printed. Bottrigari, who cared little about it, kept putting him off by promises and fine words, but finally allowed himself to be persuaded to publish this *Dialogue* without the name of an author so that he might remain in the background and hear what the world might say about it. Messer Annibale copied the Dialogue from the original manuscript of the Cavaliere — as he was accustomed to copy all the other things of that Gentleman, particularly those which Melone insisted upon publishing — and sent it to the publisher Pipino to be printed in Venice. By some accident which I don't understand, the printer lost that copy. Then Melone had to make another and send it. Since nowadays it is not permissible to publish anything, or to print any book without the name of the author, it was decided to publish it under an Anagram, and therefore as if by a fictitious person.

Some months after the publication of the *Dialogue* the Cavaliere, having learned that the Anagram by some means or other had become known to many people, was somewhat annoyed and had an explanation with Melone. Melone, in a letter which is still in existence, asked the Cavaliere for permission to explain the Anagram. In his reply the Cavaliere, for divers reasons, advised Melone not to do so, and to keep quiet about it. But because the desire to have his own name published kept increasing in him, and because he kept on pleading with the Cavaliere to allow him to disclose it, it was decided that the Anagram should be explained, by changing the letters around to their proper places in the printing (at first this Anagram was understood only by the Cavaliere, who invented it, by Melone, and by Sig. Fulvio Codibò); and also that in the title of the Dialogue the name and surname of the Signor Cavaliere, its real and true author, should be substituted. When the world had formed its opinion, which because of the soundness of the doctrine and solidity of the reasoning on which it was based could only have been a favorable one, Bottrigari was willing to permit this. So now one thing has been accomplished by the present explanation and the other by the plan which has been carried out; for, Dear Reader, I have told you this story with no other purpose than the one I have stated: to reveal the true author of IL DESIDERIO and to publish it.

DIALOGUE

Speakers: Gratioso Desiderio and Alemanno Benelli

Gr. This encounter, Messer Alemanno, at this hour and place, fills me with the greatest hopes of good fortune.

Al. And why hopes of good fortune, Signor Gratioso? You know that I honor you as a Gentleman, and that I esteem you not only as one fond of *virtuosi* (which is a kind of virtue), but as a *virtuoso* yourself.

Gr. I desire above all that we leave aside ceremony and insincere words as exaggerated and unfruitful; and for the many praises which you have given me I briefly return the greatest thanks that I can and should. But I will tell you gladly why I have placed such great hopes of good fortune on our meeting today — if perhaps I do not interrupt you in some of your business nor detain you from your journey.

Al. I left my house not for business but with the intention of hearing a great concert of music, which I learned this morning was to be given in your neighborhood shortly after luncheon, in which perhaps forty persons will participate, some playing various instruments, some singing. But I know that when a group of people must be assembled, particularly such a large number, the concert is usually late; for that reason it had almost slipped my mind. Indeed, I would have forgotten it very easily if sleep, which in these hot days usually assails the eyes of men of leisure after luncheon and which had attacked my eyes strongly, had not made me remember it. So I, fleeing it not very hastily, am now on my way.

Gr. Here is the beginning of my good fortune, M. Alemanno. The concert, for which you left your house, has already taken place; and I, having heard it through from beginning to end, am returning to my house with such renewed and increased confusion in my mind that I am not at all certain how it can be cleared up unless you, who are most intelligent and perfect in the art, and belong to the profession, liberate me (as I had told you I hoped you would), or at least give me some good solution and some help.

Al. I am very sorry to be so tardy in leaving my house that the Concert is over. But I am even more sorry that because of this concert you feel such inward confusion that you desire to find some remedy for it, and particularly from me, for I am of no help.

Gr. Do not, by speaking thus, do yourself such a great injustice, and contradict, I will not say the judgment of everyone but only mine in particular; for perhaps by this means you seek to escape giving me the hoped for, requested, and expected immediate remedy when nothing else stands in the way except your being busy.

Al. Truly I have no other business for today, for it is almost a holiday. Therefore, I offer myself wholly to anything you desire.

Gr. Would it please you then (and here my good fortune continues) to turn back twenty paces so that we can enter my house. There, by removing these cloaks and sitting down, we can be cooler, and with greater comfort talk together about what I will try to explain to you of this confusion of mine.

Al. Let us do as seems best to you.

Gr. If you please, let us go into this room, for beneath this loggia it ought to be cooler because it opens into the courtyard; nevertheless, because the sun is overcast it is hot. Do sit down, M. Alemanno, if it please you to follow my example. Let me relieve you of your cloak, even though nowadays they make them of such cloth as may be said to be spider's web. I will bring some wine and water so that you may refresh yourself; here are fans also.

Al. Please do not; for both these things would be contrary to my desires. You would have to order them, and the servants are either dispersed or napping.

Gr. Do at least sit down.

Al. I will, gladly.

Gr. First of all, M. Alemanno, since I lately encountered you, and before I saw you again, I was going along indulging in fancies in which several other times I have indulged. They were to this effect: having gone a number of times to hear various and diverse musical concerts by voices accompanied by different instruments, I have never experienced the great pleasure which I had imagined and supposed, and which, in fact I had hoped to experience. And today particularly, when I attended this one, such was the case; because, having seen a great apparatus of different kinds of instruments — among them a large Clavicembalo and a large Spinet, three Lutes of various forms, a great number of Viols and a similar large group of Trombones, two little Rebecs and as many large Flutes, straight and traverse, a large Double Harp and a Lyre — all for accompanying many good voices — there where I had thought I would hear a celestial harmony I heard confusion rather than the contrary, accompanied by a discordance, which has offended me rather than given me pleasure. Therefore, I should like you to tell me if this comes from my sense of hearing, which may not be a good judge, or if what I thought I heard is music.

Al. I understand what you are talking about, for the judgment of your senses is perfect, not only good, in the discernment of things musical. And if you heard discord rather than concord, and confusion rather than union, this may well be so. The explanation is that very often the instruments are not well tuned together, and can cause nothing but poor concord and disunity, as you have remarked.

Gr. You are right; poor concordance of the instruments can cause this. But in the concert which I heard today I do not believe that it proceeded from that cause, since all the musicians who were performing are excellent artists. I know them well, and all are capable of acting as conductors, as sometimes I have seen them do in similar concerts. Therefore I hold that there must be some other reason; and if you who are of that profession do not know it I will consider myself just as expert in music as you. Therefore, you must give me another reason.

Al. Since you press me to say what I think about it, I will tell you what I have heard experts say and what I have learned from serious writers, and will attempt to satisfy you as best I can. And if you don't grasp everything you must be content with my intentions. I have already told you that discord can arise from ill-tuned instruments, that is, the diligence which is customary in tuning the instruments together has not been observed so that they cannot make a good concord. But discord can occur for still another reason, which is this: since you have told me there were a great number of Viols, I answer you that it takes a good bit of work to make the Viols, all of which are in one group, accord well together. It is because the strings do not have any fixed stability, as we know from the testimony of Boethius in his *Musica* [a], and of Ptolemy in his *Harmonics* [b], and the same is true of the Lutes. Also because you have told me that there was a large Clavicembalo and a large Spinet, I will say that in this case too some disorder could arise, but not so much because their strings are of metal (which do not suffer much alteration, as do those of gut) as from their not being in as perfect accord as one would like. You might reply, as you have already, by saying that these instruments being in the hands of intelligent men each of them should be able to tune it properly. You would be right, if another irregularity did not arise, which is that all these virtuosi (as you will not deny) are not of the same judgment and hearing. It happens frequently that one

[a] Bk. I, Ch. 10.
[b] Bk. I, Ch. 8.

voice or one string of an instrument appears weak, or low, to one player, and to another it appears to be stretched, or high, so that the mixing of various judgments rapidly becomes confusion; so one person only should tune all the instruments. But, as Aristoxenus has said in his *Harmonic Elements,* and as Gaudentius confirms in his *Institutione Armonica* [c], one who desires an understanding of these things should above all have a practiced ear and much experience, and should understand intonation properly; that he should know the intervals, and finally, that he should know what are consonances and dissonances. Aristoxenus gives these maxims at the end of his preface. Another thing, of no little importance, is that among those instruments which you have named there are several kinds; hence, some are entirely stable, others are stable but alterable. In addition there are still others of various different species.

Gr. To tell the truth, M. Alemanno, I do not understand these different kinds of instruments, nor what may be an entirely stable instrument, nor what you mean by a "stable but alterable instrument", nor "entirely mobile instruments"; nor do I know their various species.

Al. I will tell you. The stable instruments are those which, after they have been tuned by a conscientious Maestro, cannot be altered by any means. Such are Organs, Harpsichords, Spinets, Double Harps, and other similar instruments, which can produce only the pure diatonic scale which pleases most people, or seems to please them. The stable but alterable instruments are all those which, after they have been tuned by the diligent player, can be changed, augmented or diminished in some degree, according to the good judgment of the player as he touches their frets a little higher or a little lower. This occurs with the Lute and Viol, even though they may have the stability of their frets. The same thing happens with the wind instruments, such as straight and traverse Flutes and straight and curved Cornetts. Even though they may have a certain stability because of their holes, the accomplished player can nonetheless use a little less or a little more breath and can open the vents a little more or a little less, bringing them closer to a good accord. Expert players do this. The instruments which are completely alterable are those which have neither fingerboards nor holes — Trombones, Ribechini, Lire, and the like. These, having ordinarily neither frets nor openings, can wander here and there, according to the will of the player, and can be limited by lengthening or shortening the "draws" (as the tubes of the Trombone are called) or by the loosening or tightening of the lips. And likewise

c Chap. I.

with the Lira and the Ribechini the tone can be altered by touching the strings over the neck either higher or lower, at the will and pleasure of the player.

I have already told you that among these instruments there are various species; so the Organ, the Clavicembalo, the Spinet, and others like them, are of the same species and they sound, as pleases some people, the syntonic diatonic of Ptolemy, tempered however, or divided, according to the custom of the expert makers and tuners of such instruments. Ptolemy's diatonic, among all the diatonics called "first genus" by Aristoxenus in his *Harmonics,* is more natural than the other genera and is nearest to the sense and reason of those who up to the present have been trained in music. The Lutes and Viols have another kind (of diatonic), the same for both of them, which is said by some writers to be Aristoxenus' species of intense diatonic [1] because the tones are divided into two equal semitones (which is the opinion of that same Aristoxenus). One hears and sees this in the Lutes and Viols.

The wind instruments with openings, such as the straight and traverse Flutes, straight and curved Cornetts, and others like them, are all one species using the syntonic diatonic of Ptolemy more often than not. Since they cannot possess exact certainty either by the openings or by the breath (as Ptolemy affirms in his *Harmonics* [d]), we shall pass over them. Nevertheless, I will add that I have spoken with excellent makers of such instruments and I find that they do not have anything firm on which to base a solid argument, but when they bore the holes of such instruments they depend only on their ear, aided by nature, broadening the openings as the need is felt. Such was the custom of the ancient makers of Tibias and Fistulas, as we read in the writings on music of Ptolemy and Aristoxenus [e].

The instruments which are entirely alterable, the Trombones and Ribechini, can sound not only the three harmonic genera but also each and every species of these genera, which are 24 — six kinds of enharmonic, eight kinds of chromatic, and ten of diatonic, as may

d Bk. I, Ch. 8. Bk. II, Ch. 12.
e Ch. 12 of Bk. II; a little before the middle of Bk. II.

---

1 Bottrigari uses most often the expression "diatonico incitato" for this particular species. "Incitato" means pushed, or stretched, or taut; therefore I take Bottrigari's use of the term to be his equivalent of σύντονον, or intense diatonic, as implied by Aristoxenus. (Cf. Mountford's discussion of the two varieties of diatonic in "A New Fragment of Greek Music in Cairo", *Journal of Hellenic Studies,* LI (1931), 91. Cf. also, C. V. Palisca, *Girolamo Mei: Letters on Ancient and Modern Music* (Am. Inst. of Musicology, 1960) pp. 69, 158.

be seen more clearly in the special tables described by Ptolemy in his *Harmonics*[f]; and in addition they can sound all our modern Harmonic species, and every other which has been or may have been newly invented.

I have already said that the stable instruments use the syntonic diatonic of Ptolemy, and some of the others, stable but alterable (i.e. straight and traverse Flutes, straight and curved Cornetts and others like them) sound the same diatonic more often than any other, but that some other stable but alterable ones, such as Lutes, Viols and others similar, sound the intense diatonic of Aristoxenus, or of some other ancient writer. Therefore I do not wish either to affirm or deny, or even to dispute, whether or not the semitone said to be minor is minor, or if indeed it has a position between the greatest and the least; it will suffice to demonstrate by its effects — i.e. the Clavicembalo, the Organ, and their like, sound two unequal semitones, one larger than the other. The Lute and the Viols sound two equal semitones, that is, a tone divided into two equal semitones according to the idea of Aristoxenus.

To clarify the matter further, since I have told you that even though I could adduce the authority of several excellent modern writers on music[g], I wish nonetheless for your sense of hearing to make you certain about it, and that we should by experiment demonstrate which instruments of various species can be united and tuned well together. Therefore, it will be well if we go over to that Clavicembalo and see and hear whether or not the things I have been telling you are true.

Since I believe that it is well-tuned, as well as those other instruments which I see arranged around here, I will ask you now to take one of those Lutes and tune it with all possible accuracy in accord with the Clavicembalo in the following manner. I will touch the G sol re ut on the Clavicembalo. Now you tune the open tenor course of your Lute in unison with me, and then tune the remainder according to the rule, as I know you are able to do.

Gr. There, it's tuned.

Al. Now I strike the E la mi on the Clavicembalo. Touch the E la

[f] Bk. II, Ch. 14.

[g] Don Nic. Vicentino in the last Chap. of his *Ancient and Modern Music;* Galilei in his *Dialogue* on music; Zarlino in Chap. 27 of part 4 of his *Sopplimenti musicali;* Salinas in Chap. 28 of the 3rd part and throughout.

mi on your Lute, which will be the open *Mezanina*[2]. Are you tuned and in unison with the E la mi of the Clavicembalo?

Gr. We are.

Al. Now I play F fa ut on the Cembalo. Now touch your F fa ut on the first fret of the *Mezanina* of your Lute. Are you tuned in unison with me?

Gr. We are not.

Al. Now I touch the G sol re ut on the Clavicembalo and you touch the G sol re ut at the third fret of the *Mezanina*. Are you tuned in unison with me, that is with the Clavicembalo?

Gr. We are.

Al. Now I touch the raised G sol re ut on the Clavicembalo. Touch the fourth fret of the *Mezanina* to obtain the diesis of G sol re ut. Are you in unison and tuned with the Clavicembalo?

Gr. No, we are not. And what causes that, M. Alemanno?

Al. I will tell you; but what you have heard in the *Mezanina* happens with all the other strings each time you touch the semitones.

Gr. From what does that proceed?

Al. Have I not told you that the Clavicembalo and such instruments sound one species, and the Lute and its like sound another?

Gr. You have.

Al. If then these instruments are of two different species, how can you expect them to unite perfectly together?

Gr. You tell me, and make me see and hear, things that I would never have believed. But now that I both see and hear I can only confess that you speak truly.

Al. It should not seem so important not to know these things, since people who work at them all day and put their energies into arranging such groups of instruments (concerti) do not understand it either. That much is clear, because if they knew it and understood it they would not make such "concerts", or rather such "confusions". Therefore, having the tone divided into two equal semitones, as do the Lutes and Viols, while the Clavicembalo and its kind have it divided in two unequal semitones, it happens that when I sound F fa ut on the Clavicembalo and you touch F fa ut at the first fret of the *Mezanina* of the Lute, you do not find yourself in unison with me,

[2] The string is miscalled; it should be *Sottana*. The A tuning of the Italian lute was the following: Basso, A; Bordone, D; Tenore, G; Mezzana (or Mezzanina), b; Sottana, e; Canto, a. Therefore the open string referred to which sounds E la mi can only be the Sottana; likewise, only the Sottana could sound the G sol re ut at the 3rd fret.

as you both heard and admitted. The reason is this, that the Clavicembalo sounds the greater semitone, which is divided in the proportion of 16 : 15, or somewhat more than a half tone; and the Lute sounds the semitone divided equally, which happens to be smaller than the greater semitone of 16 to 15, which is larger than a half tone. And when I played the raised G sol re ut on the Clavicembalo, you played the G sol re ut raised at the fourth fret of the *Mezanina* string of the Lute; we did not find ourselves in unison, as you heard and stated. This happens because the Clavicembalo sometimes sounds the tempered semitone called minor, which is in the proportion of *sesquiventiquatresima,* or 25 to 24, considerably less than a half tone. And the Lute (when I say Lute I mean Lutes, Viols, and similar instruments) plays the equally divided half-tone, which happens to be somewhat greater than that semitone called minor, in the proportion of 25 to 24. It is no wonder that we do not find ourselves in unison at that place, and it will be the same in all the other places where such a difference and diversity of semitones occurs.

I will give you still another explanation to show that the semitones of the aforesaid instruments are not equal. The players of the entirely stable instruments, as the Clavicembalo, Organ, and others, however excellent they may be, when they wish to transpose a tone lower or higher, or a semitone lower or higher, cannot do so in all places on their instrument. And here is the reason. When it is necessary to play the semitone commonly called major, since they lack it on their instruments they must needs play the one commonly called minor, whence the auditors and they themselves feel that their sense of hearing is offended. Expert players of such instruments and those who are skilled in music know this very well. But the same thing does not happen with the Lute and Viol, because they always have the equal semitone and can transpose a tone higher or lower, and a semitone higher or lower, without offending the ear. It is done continually by expert players when they make a bridge, as they say, at the first or second fret with the index finger of the left hand, or wherever it best suits them (close to the frets, however, so that the auditory sense is not offended), and thus play as if it were the beginning of the neck [3].

[3] The usual term for this practice is *barré.*

Gr. That is true; I have seen it done many times. But from what you tell me and from what we are discussing, it would seem not possible to play together (*far concerti*) [4].

Al. On the contrary; because of what we are discussing we *are* able to play together (*fare concerti*).

Gr. What enigmatic speech is this! Would it please you to explain it to me, for I do not understand.

Al. I have said that people can all the better play together; for if you will investigate what the word *concerto* means, you will find that, as I have said and repeat, they can indeed make a *concerto,* for *concerto* means "contention" or "conflict" — on which point we have the testimony of Cicero in the oration *Pro lege manilia,* and in the letter to Atticus, and in the book *De natura deorum,* and in the beginning of *De divinatione;* also of Terence in the second scene of the second act of the *Adelphi;* and I would mention Pliny if I remembered the place rightly. Therefore those who make such *concerti* do indeed observe the etymology of the word.

Gr. We are joking and jesting. And if we should place an "s" instead of the "c" in the word *concerto* as we use it, and present it in the Florentine manner, and perhaps that of all Tuscany, *conserto,* as a word derived from the verb *consero,* which means to join together or to graft, to sow and plant together, which verb Virgil used in the second of his *Georgics* (if I remember aright), and in the first of the *Eclogues,* Columella in the twenty-first book, and Cicero in the *Toscolane,* in the book *De natura deorum* and elsewhere, would not your joking and your burlesqued problem be pointless?

Al. In no other way would it become pointless; but there would be little gained, inasmuch as, to my way of thinking, *conserto* is used by the Tuscans rather as a habit (not to say a bad habit) of their pronunciation in similar words than because it may have your derivation. *Consero, conseris,* which has that meaning of sowing, planting and grafting together, gives *consevi, consitum,* and not *conservi, consertum* as does the other *consero, conseris* — from which *consertus* is truly derived. This would be the proper word, not only in Tuscan but in our Italian, *conserto,* which means to "skirmish", "to come to blows", in short, "to contend in public places", as with weapons, if we give credence, as we should, to the authority of Cicero in the *Toscolane*

[4] On this subject see D. Boyden's article "When is a Concerto not a Concerto?" *Musical Quarterly,* XLIII, no. 2 (April 1957), 220; and R. A. Hall, Jr.'s further discussion in *Italica,* XXXV, no. 3 (Sept. 1958), 188 "Italian 'Concerto' ('Conserto') and 'Concerto' ".

(which you mentioned), in the letter to Atticus, and also in the orations *Pro Murena* and *Pro Funteio;* and to that of Virgil in the second book of his *Aeneid,* and to that of Nonius Marcellus, the grammarian, and, in conclusion, to all the commentators. You need not therefore marvel if you hear these discords and confusion.

Gr. You are continuing your joking. I ask you whether or not people can concertize together; however, I mean can they make a good and beautiful concert together.

Al. If they played beautifully and well together it should be neither *concerti* nor *conserti,* but *concenti.* And as for this harmony, I hold that it can be done with some effort; otherwise the letter "n" will be changed to "r" or "s", and in place of *concento* they will have *concerto* or *conserto.* However, in our discussion we will use *concerto* and *concento* interchangeably so as not to depart from our ordinary manner of speech.

Gr. But how will they achieve these *concenti*?

Al. I will tell you as best I can, always referring to those who understand better than I (as the good jurist says) in this or any other matter. But first, Sig. Gratioso, be good enough to consider what concept the "Master of those who know," Aristotle, might have of such modern musical concerts[h]; and how could he allow them, since he, resolving a proposition on the accompaniment of the human voice by a Lyre alone, or by a single Tibia, said (if I remember correctly) these exact words: "But with more instruments its sweetness cannot be preserved, inasmuch as the melody becomes obscured and almost entirely destroyed." Since it is almost as if I had made this statement myself I will say that such *concerti* can be made when one understands the nature of the instruments which are to be used together. Therefore, when one has knowledge and uses it, *concenti* can be made in many and diverse manners, to the greatest advantage. But one must know well how to arrange and unite the instruments. And if the usual species of stable instruments are taken and played together (Organs, Clavicembali, Spinets, and the like) there is no doubt that if they are well-tuned (which, in my opinion, is no easy matter) they will sound in that perfection which instruments artificially tempered, or divided, can achieve. And we have had experience of this, for there are many chamber organs which have Clavicembali joined with them and which sound together to the great delight and pleasure of the hearer, especially when they have more than one kind of register of pipes or strings.

[h] Prob. 9, sec. 19.

Concenti may also be formed by entirely stable instruments (Organs, Clavicembali and the like) together with instruments entirely alterable, Trombones, Ribechini, and human voices. This is because the latter are capable, as we have said above, of uniting with any species whatsoever; the voices and instruments must be warned, however, to accord with the stable instruments, which cannot possibly change in any way from where they were first tuned.

Ensembles can also be made with stable instruments (as Organs, Clavicembali, Harps and the like) and with stable-alterable ones, such as Lutes and Viols. But we have already proved that the stable and stable-alterable cannot unite perfectly because they sound different species (of scales), and the greatest cause of this is the difference of the semitones. However, as we have said before, the stable-alterable instruments, which are Lutes, Viols, straight and traverse Flutes, straight and curved Cornetts, would be of no value if one could not use their alterations in some degree, nor would we call them "stable-alterable". We must make a division of these, separating the ones with strings and frets from those that have openings and are blown; because, as we have said, they are of a different species both as to sound and genus. Whence, speaking first about the vented wind instruments, because in their sound they are almost the same as those which are stable, we will conclude that one can make them play together in the following way: each time that a tone is to be played by the stable instruments the diligent player of the stable-alterable wind instrument will accord with the stable instrument by carefully using a little more or a little less breath, and by opening or closing the holes of his instrument a little more or less according to his will and need. As to the strings with frets, as Lutes, Viols, the good player, after he has taken the tone or sound from the stable instruments, will have some difficulty in coming to a good unison with them because of the difference in species and genus, as we have said. But he will be able, with diligent application, to do so, helping himself by placing the finger a little higher or a little lower on the fingerboard when he feels the need.

There remains to speak of combining all these species of instruments — stable as well as stable-alterable and entirely alterable. But since I hold that this cannot be done except with the greatest disunion, such as you heard today and described to me, I would advise you never to make such an orchestra, for it can only be done with the greatest difficulty, and is next to impossible.

The reason is this; when one combines the stable-alterable instruments, which are of two different species (that is, strings with frets and wind with vents), with the entirely alterable and the entirely stable, even if each player of stable-alterable instruments makes every effort to unite with the stable and the entirely alterable, they can never be in complete accord; because when they try to unite with those of wind, vented, (as being the ones which can most easily adapt themselves, being nearest to the fixed) they can never perfectly agree with those of strings and frets (the most difficult to accord with the entirely stable). And on the contrary, the entirely alterable ones, when they try to be in tune with the alterable ones of strings and frets, will become farther away from the others of wind, and so produce a real *concerto,* or battle, of instruments, instead of a *concento,* a union and concord of diverse voices and sounds. So, if one wishes to double or triple the parts of a chorus one should take (according to my way of thinking) the greatest care never to mate instruments of different species; that is, winds with strings. If, for example, one wished to duplicate the Tenor parts one should never use a Flute or a great Cornett, or an instrument of a species other than a Viol or Lute; because the manifest disunion or discord would be too clearly revealed. And we are justified in giving such advice for, by contrary sense, one can refer in a way to the words of Aristoxenus, even to Ptolemy in his *Harmonics,* where he advises that one should always couple the Tibia or Fistula with the ancient monochord; and the practice is judged by Aristotle, in his *Problems* [i], to be of great importance. To this very important warning I think it best to add that no concert of instruments should ever be given without the addition of a human voice — always a voice well suited to the subject of the song. This is to avoid the music and the concert being called "mute" by connoisseurs and intelligent listeners, or as Aristotle calls it, and Plato [j] calls it more clearly and better in the *Laws,* the "bare" sound of the Cithara or the Aulos, which they say resembles the sounds made by animals. This is because of the failure to express the *affetti* and because of the poor pronunciation of the words. From the words, especially when they are well mimed by a good musician, truly comes the greater part of the emotions aroused in the minds of the listeners.

Gr. I would like to ask two things which I have delayed asking until now in order not to impede the progress of your discourse. The first is this — many times I have heard you speak of tempered or divided instruments, and since I don't understand what these tempered in-

i At the end of Ch. 1 of Bk. II. Prob. 44, sec. 19.

j At the end of the last Bk. of the Politics. Much clearer and fuller, and very much better, in Plato, somewhat past the middle of the sec. on Laws.

struments signify I would like for you to make it clear to me. The other is, that I am astonished that so many men, held to be of good judgment, in forming ensembles have never been aware of the discord of which we have spoken. I can bring myself only with difficulty to give credence to your words, however sure I feel that all you have been telling me is true and reasonably demonstrated.

Al. I will answer in the order of your questions, and will say that the tempering of the stable and stable-alterable instruments was, I do not know whether to say, rediscovered by study or happened accidentally [k]. Nowadays it is usual to avoid a plurality or multiplicity of strings, both for the convenience of the players and in order to make the instruments easier to play together (for to unite is impossible, as you have understood) — that is, the stable with the stable-alterable and the alterable with the stable — without much offence and annoyance, or rather affront, to the auditory sense. Now, as to your other question about *concerti,* I will say . . .

Gr. Easy now, M. Alemanno. You said that tempering is an avoidance of strings in the stable instruments, whereby you almost demonstrate that there may be instruments with a greater number of strings than are now found in Organs, Clavicembali, Harps, and the like.

Al. When I say "plurality of strings" [l] I do not mean to say what is seen nowadays in instruments such as Organs, Clavicembali and the like, where are found 45 or more keys and strings or pipes, because such a plurality is nothing more than a duplication or triplication of the first perfect system, that is, of the fifteen strings of the syntonic diatonic as conceived by Ptolemy. Nor do I mean by true plurality of strings what is obtained by the further division of the Tetrachord synemmenon, nor a kind of chromatic, that is, the tones or sounds raised, as they say, with the *diesis,* which means that one leaves one genus, the diatonic, and enters the chromatic, a thing which is found also today in stable instruments.

But by the plurality of strings and pipes [m] it seems to me that one must understand it to be a system which enables one to have all the consonances in their perfect proportion. These consonances are: the *diapente,* or fifth, in the proportion *sesquialtera;* the *diatessaron,*

[k] How tempering of musical instruments came about; Reasons for tempering musical instruments.

[l] 45 or more keys in organs, clavicembali & like instruments; apparent plurality of strings nothing other than duplication of notes of the perfect system.

[m] What true plurality of strings is; to have all the consonances in their true form & proportion.

or fourth, in the proportion *sesquiterza;* the *ditone,* or let us say, major third, in the proportion *sesquiquarta;* the *semiditone,* or minor third, in the proportion *sesquiquinta;* the major hexachord, or major sixth, in the proportion *superbipartienteterza,* which is from 5 to 3; and the minor hexachord, or minor sixth, in the proportion *supertripartientequinta,* that is from 8 to 5. As to the Diapason, or octave [n], which is in the proportion *dupla,* there need be no question, for of this (consonance) there is not made, nor can there be made, any alteration whatever, in order not to alter or spoil or destroy every constitution or multiplicity of pipes or strings in the aforesaid instruments.

The multiplicity of strings arises from the fact that in the system of Ptolemy, in the syntonic diatonic as now used, a long fourth and a short fifth [o] is found within the space of a Diapason, that is, between the string Proslambanomenos, or let us say A re, and Mese, or a la mi re. The long fourth occurs between the string *Proslambanomenos* A re and the *Lichanos Hypaton,* or D sol re; and between this D sol re and the *Mese,* or a la mi re, the short fifth. Their difference is the modern comma which is contained in the proportion *sesquiottantesima,* or 81 to 80. Therefore, in order to have these consonances in their perfect proportion and form it would be necessary to add a string below the D sol re to make a true fifth with a la mi re and a true fourth with A re [p]. This added D sol re would be the D sol re of the old diatonic. Besides this, to gain the minor third with F fa ut, and for the ditone, or major third with low b fa, it would be necessary also to add still another string between the B mi and the low b fa, which is the 8ve of the string b fa above the *Mese* A la, called by the ancients *Tritesynemmenon,* and is the third of the tetrachord synemmenon with which it is joined. From this comes the increase of the number of strings which we have previously put in the second place together with the increase of the syntonic diatonic genus by the chromatic genus. And with the added string of the second b fa one would have the true ditone [q], or major third, with the D sol re, in the proportion *sesquiquarta,* that is, 5 to 4; whereas now the usual b fa gives the old ditone which is in the proportion *superpartientedecisettesessantaquatresima,* that is 81 to 64, and is therefore called by all the ancient writers the dissonant interval, as one reads in the

n Diapason or octave never undergoes alteration.

o Long fourth and short fifth in octave of Ptolemy's syntonic diatonic system, beginning with Proslambanomenos, that is, A re: Proportion of the modern comma.

p Added D sol re gives the true fifth between A la mi re and the minor third with F fa ut, & with lower B fa, the ditone.

q Added B fa gains the ditone or major third with D sol re, and the semiditone, or minor third, with Gamma ut.

Harmonic Elements of Aristoxenus [r]. Ptolemy, in his *Harmonics,* says that because it is dissonant it is not suitable for song. With this string one would have the semiditone, or minor third with Gamma Ut. All this matter appears much more clearly in the *Musica speculativa* of Lodovico Fogliano, the first writer, as far as I know, to reason soundly about it.

Gr. If you please, M. Alemanno, would you kindly restrain the course of your speech and clarify several things for me which seem very obscure because I have never done any theoretical study in matters of music, but have only paid attention to the pleasure and delight afforded my sense of hearing by the composition and sound, as is the usual practice in our time. And if I were willing to delay my understanding of these things until the end of your discourse I am almost certain that I would forget the greater part, and I don't want to forget even one thing.

Al. It makes no difference to me if you interrupt me in my discourse because everything comes back to that one thread, since in our talk we are not using a scientific method or order in matters of music but are only talking about them for your instruction.

Gr. A plurality of strings, I am convinced does not mean 45 or more keys and like number of strings or pipes which one sees in the instruments. I understand no more than this, if indeed there is anything more to be understood; each time one passes the Diapason, or 8ve, one must always return to the beginning, that is, it would be higher or lower by one octave, according to the position where first one started.

Al. Perfectly correct; but I must inform you that there is indeed no perfect system until you reach the Disdiapason, that is, to the *quadrupla* or *quintadecima,* because then not only are there the seven species of Diapason, and the four species of the Diapente and the three species of the Diatessaron, as Ptolemy shows us in his *Harmonics* [s], but all the other consonances as well — that is the major tenth in the proportion 5 to 2, and the minor tenth, in the proportion 12 to 5, and the twelfth, which is in triple proportion of 3 to 1; also the diapason diatessaron, or let us say 11th, in *proportio dupla superbipartienteterza,* that is 8 to 3, and finally the 15th or Disdiapason in *proportio quadrupla,* or 4 to 1. And this must be understood as the

r At the end of the first chapter of the first book of Aristoxenus; near the middle of the 2. Chapter 2 of the 3 divisions.

s Bk. II, Ch. 4. Proportions of the Compound consonances.

complete and perfect constitution (of the system) in its true form, since after this one really begins again.

Gr. I understand. But when you say that you do not mean true plurality of strings and pipes by that which is contained in the further division of the Tetrachord synemmenon, and by one chromatic genus, please tell me first of all what the Tetrachord synemmenon is. After that, what that Chromatic genus may be; and finally, why this should not be a true plurality of strings or pipes since it seems to me that it should be a true plurality, because it contains a crowding together into which many and different kinds of strings and pipes enter.

Al. The Tetrachord synemmenon, for such words signify four conjunct strings, is a Tetrachord added to the first two, which are from *Hypate hypaton,* to *Hypate meson,* that is, from B mi to E la mi; and from *Hypate meson* to *Mese,* that is, from E la mi to the second a la mi re. To this *Mese,* (that is, a la mi re) is added a third Tetrachord which, beginning at the *Mese,* or a la mi re, goes to *Netesynemmenon,* that is d la sol re; one cannot proceed beyond this conjunctively, as Ptolemy demonstrates in his *Harmonics*[t]. The place of the Tetrachords in such instruments (as the Clavicembalo) are after the first three successive black keys, called semitones, and then four keys higher; and then another three. That is, from ♮ mi to E la mi, and from E la mi then three keys higher to a la mi re; from this a la mi re ascending three keys higher you will arrive at d la sol re, excluding however the succeeding white key and using instead the third black key, calling it b fa.

Gr. Would you show me these things on the Cembalo, since we have it here, so that with greater clearness I can easily comprehend the whole.

Al. You see here, these are the first three successive black keys.

Gr. So they are.

Al. This first white key is ♮ mi, where we begin the Tetrachords, as I have said. The following is C fa ut, the third D sol re, the fourth E la mi; and following this E la mi is F fa ut, and this other the key of G sol re ut, and this other a la mi re, which make the second Tetrachord.

Now, starting from this a la mi re and touching the third of these three black keys we have b fa, and skipping this next white, which is the higher octave of ♮ mi, we will pass to the next successive white which is c fa ut, and finally we shall come to the following white, which is d la sol re — which completes, so to speak, the three conjunct Tetrachords, or the Tetrachord synemmenon.

[t] Bk. II, Ch. 6.

Gr. Tell me, why do you select that semitone which you call b fa and leave the white ♮ mi in making the conjunction of the three Tetrachords?

Al. The reason is this: because from A re to ♮ mi is a Tone, when you wish to make this conjunction it is necessary that it be a Semitone and not a Tone. On the other hand, beginning with the first of the three Tetrachords, that is with ♮ mi, and rising one note it makes a Semitone to C fa ut; and from C fa ut to D sol re, a Tone; and from D sol re to E la mi, another Tone; and this is the first Tetrachord. The other two following are formed in a similar manner. However, from this E la mi to that F fa ut is a Semitone, and from F fa ut to G sol re ut, a Tone; and from G sol re ut to a la mi re, a Tone. Likewise at this a la mi re, wishing to add the third Tetrachord, it is necessary that the Semitone follow and not the Tone, which makes it go then from a la mi re to b fa; and after this follows the whole step, that is from b fa to c sol fa ut, and from that c sol fa ut to d la sol re another step; and these are the three conjunct Tetrachords.

But you should know also that the tone we have between a la mi re and ♮ mi is called the tone of division or disjunction, because here the first two lower or inferior tetrachords, the first of which is called Hypaton and the second Meson, are disjoined and separated from the other two higher Tetrachords, the first of which is called Diezeugmenon, that is, 'disjoined', and the second Hyperbolaion, that is, 'excellent'. Diezeugmenon consists of ♮ mi, C sol fa ut, D la sol re, E la mi; and the Hyperbolaion of e la mi, f fa ut, g sol re ut, a la mi re. In these the same order is continued as we have mentioned for the low or inferior ones — that is by semitone, tone, and tone, which is always mi fa sol la. The Hand of Guido, the monk of Arezzo, gives us clear information about this matter.

Gr. These speculations are too deep for me to be able to learn them immediately; nonetheless, I feel a certain pleasure in them. But before we go farther, tell me, please, why have you omitted those first three white keys, which you haven't mentioned at all? And why are they in the instrument and, so to speak, the foundation of it?

Al. I have not mentioned them because they are all octaves of the higher tones, as we have seen. This one, just before ♮ mi, is called by modern musicians A re; but the ancients called it *proslambanomenos,* that is 'acquired', or added as the octave of a la mi re. Therefore the Mese, represented by that a la mi re, was truly placed in the middle of the perfect system, and was also called *prosmelodos,* as

Boethius [u] tells us repeatedly. Hence one sees that the Tetrachords should truly have their beginning at ♮ mi — where indeed we began. This other key next in order is called Gamma Ut, for it also is a string added by less ancient musicians for the octave of G sol re ut, as Guido D'Arezzo says in the beginning of his *Micrologus musicale* [v]. He used it to make his hexachords complete, that is, ut, re, mi, fa, sol, la. And this first key is called F fa ut, or octave of that other f fa ut. And as these notes can be increased in highness to infinity, so to infinity can they be made lower, if the spirit is not lacking, either in the one or the other extremity. Aristoxenus has written profoundly about this in his *Harmonic Elements.*

Gr. Would you be good enough to tell me again about these black keys, or semitones, both the first ones and the others following, for you haven't spoken of them at all.

Al. These (and this will also reply to the other part of the multiplicity of strings you have asked me about, which is what the chromatic genus or species may be) are the tones which present-day musicians term "raised" and indicate by one of their characters they have called "diesis", whose form is this ♯, as you know. And they call them semitones, but improperly, because they are not truly a half-tone. Some of these are indicated also with the b fa, as we have said, which is always a wide semitone. Beginning with that black semitone next to C fa ut, we will say it is C fa ut raised, and this other E la mi with the flat; that first black note of the second three is F fa ut raised, and the second one is G sol re ut raised; the third you already know, for we have said that it is the b fa of the synemmenon. All these others above, as all the others below, are octaves of these, as we have seen.

Gr. I understand that perfectly. But I should like to know why in many Clavicembali and Organs, as I have noticed, these first two semitones or black keys are not found, but only this third one of b fa.

Al. I think that may be done because such raised keys in the bass are seldom used. Rather, as you must have noticed, the modern makers of Clavicembali and Organs tune them in octaves with D sol re and E la mi, and then add a white key below that lowest F fa ut and, tuning it an octave below C fa ut, they say they provide the mi, re, ut. But when, however, they use the first two black keys for the purpose of raised octaves there is nothing else to do but tune the added white key in its proper octave with E la mi, so that it does not remain idle.

[u] Bk. I, Ch. 20, 22.

[v] Not far from the beginning & also a little before the middle of Bk. I.

Nor do I wish to pass over in silence a thing of no little importance which almost none of the present day practical musicians know about. It is, that having in their compositions called by them "per b-molle" [with a flat], which is the species of the three conjunct Tetrachords, that is, of the Synemmenon, having established the b fa and wishing to raise it to make the major third or tenth with the G sol re ut, or with the Gamma ut, and also to avoid the false fifth with E la mi, they indicate that b fa with the diesis (♯), striking and sounding the ♮ mi of the species of the disjunct tetrachords. But that of the players succeeds best when, however, it is not the string in the proportion 25 to 24, marked by some and not by others of these practical musicians with their sign of diesis with which they always indicate the minor semitone, for if they wish to properly reintegrate this ♮ mi it must be the semitone of 135 to 128, which is greater than the minor semitone by a modern comma, that is 81 to 80 [w]. Wherefore, in order to avoid such inconvenience, they ought to use not the diesis but the b quadro (♮); and thus the ♮ mi would be truly reintegrated. The reason for their defect is that they believe that in this place there should be a minor tone, and in reality it is the major, which is that of the division. This however is done very well now by them, for proceeding by *Musica finta* they place the flat (b-molle) on E la mi, and wishing then to raise, and return to that true E la mi, they place beneath this flat their diesis; inasmuch as in that place the minor tone is found, composed of the major semitone, which is the b-molle, and of the minor, which is the diesis.

Now let us speak of the character of the chromatic genus. But first you should know that modern composers and players believe that the raised tones are of the diatonic genus; however, they are not, nor of any of its species, and it has therefore no black key except the b fa, which is the major semitone. The raised tones are of the chromatic genus except, however, the raised G sol re ut which has been brought in both for the major tenth with E la mi and for the minor with ♮ mi, and because it can serve for the fifth with raised C fa ut; in sum, the raised G sol re ut is not, nor can it be, in any way part of the chromatic genus because it never had in its system this string, or tone, either artificial or raised, only the natural; unless one then proceeds by *Musica finta*.

Gr. And what is this *Musica finta*, of which you have just spoken?

[w] Difference of the minor semitone and the semitone *supersettepartientecento-ventottesimo.*

Al. *Musica finta* (for it is not "vera", since it comes outside of the true tetrachords) is an alteration of the original tetrachord by means of the semitones in the manner of the true tetrachords as if they proceeded disjunctly starting a tone lower with the major tone of division [x], which is between the Mese and the Paramese, or, let us say, a la mi re and ♮ mi acute, becoming minor between Lichanos Meson and the Mese, that is, between g sol re ut and a la mi re.

Gr. Even though I understand your reasoning with my intellect, nonetheless I would like for you to put it before my eyes by giving me an example, so that I may have a clear and complete understanding.

Al. Gladly. But for now I will give you the example of the diatonic genus, reserving for a later and more convenient place to give you an example of the chromatic; then you will understand it all. Here is the example (Ex. I) in which you see the connection of the first

Ex. I. *Musica finta* with flats, and its perfect system, the hard diatonic of Ptolemy

tetrachord to be D sol re, the second connection is d la sol re, and thus you proceed up to the acute G sol re ut. And the third tetrachord, which thus is disjunct, from Synemmenon has become Diezeugmenon by one step lower; [y] and the fourth, from d sol re to g sol re ut, does the office of Hyperbolaion. As you can see here on the Clavicembalo, beginning from A re and rising by one semitone, and then by a major tone, and then by a minor, and thus continuing in all the others.

Gr. In spite of the fact that I see well with my eyes and hear also with my ears, it doesn't seem to me that I could apply it practically if I had need. Nor could I say with certainty what *Musica finta* is.

Al. Oho, you say something which I can scarcely believe, and which seems to me impossible; that you do not remember having seen it, after I spoke to you practically about these clefs (Ex. II).

Ex. II. Clefs used for *musica finta* with flats

Gr. Certainly you have made me remember with these demonstra-

[x] Tone of disjunction which is always major in *musica vera* becomes minor in *musica finta,* and why.

[y] Tetrachord Diezeugmenon lowered by one tone in *musica finta.*

tions. And I remember having seen that famous motet of Gian Motone, *Peccata mia,* with these clefs; and that of Loyset Pieton, *O admirabile,* in which he is not content to put 3 flats (b-molli), but several times adds the fourth to A re of the Bass, and also in the Quinto to D sol re two or three times. I also recall another, of Adriano Willaert, in the *Peccorina,* which begins "Aspice Domine"; and if I'm not mistaken, the Madrigal *Ponmi ove il sol,* in the 3rd book a 5 of Cipriano.

Al. Such is indeed the case. But perhaps you have noticed that several of these tones, or flats of a la mi re, or let us say A re and D sol re, are not ordinarily found on the Clavicembali or other such instruments. You must then remember how this *Musica finta* may be reduced to *musica vera* by writing a motet or a madrigal either one tone higher with the ♮ quadro, or a fifth higher with the b molle; or, with the same b molle, a fourth lower, which is the same, but being an octave lower.

Gr. I believe I do remember, and I think it should be done in this way (Ex. III).

Ex. III

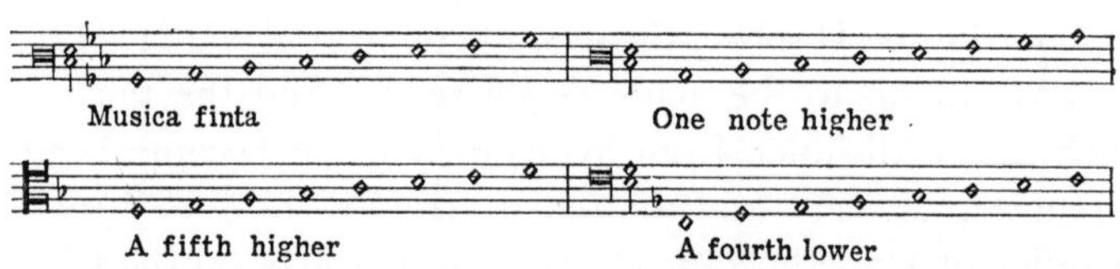

Al. You have spoken and done well. This is exactly what one has to do. But you haven't mentioned the other *Musica Finta,* not so much esteemed, either because you do not know it or do not remember it. This proceeds by minor semitones, or raised notes, as is indicated by the diesis in these forms. It is reduced to *musica vera* by raising it a semiditone and taking away the diesis (Ex. IV).

Ex. IV. *Musica finta* with sharps, and how it may be reduced to *musica vera*

Gr. I did remember it indeed, but I was trying to think of an example.

Al. You have an example by an excellent man and famous organist, Annibale Padovano, in one of his "fantasies", as the practical players say, printed in his first book of Ricercari.

Gr. That is perfectly true. In my opinion these *musiche finte* are more useful for such players than for singers or composers, unless the composers use it to train their singers. But this discussion of *Musica finta* would easily lead us to speak of that Duo of Adriano which apparently finishes on the seventh and gives musicians of these times much to think about and talk about, even to write about — among others Giovanni Spadaro who, as I understand, showed clearly in his letter written to Don Pietro Aron about this duo that he is not a second-rate musician. But I do not wish our, or rather my, anecdotes or digressions which are now so many as to be excessive, to prolong too much the conclusion of our discussion. Continue telling me about the chromatic genus, in order that you may finish explaining temperament, if you have finished with the true plurality of strings.

Al. I do not wish that anything remain to tell you about *musica finta*, unless you have not learned it before. For though in solfeggio, let us say, one uses the same names of the tones they are not always the same intervals; and especially, to mention only one, that tone which is between g sol re ut and a la mi re, used as the tone of disjunction in *musica finta* (as we have said), is minor, and in the *musica vera* the one between a la mi re and ♮ mi is major.

Gr. Good. But please do not delay the completion of the matters which remain to be explained, so that you can discuss concerti, as you have promised, and as I refuse to forget.

Al. Don't worry, we'll get to the concerti presently. However, as to the chromatic genus there remain only a few little things to be mentioned; and almost nothing about tempering after we shall have talked about the plurality of strings, because in this plurality consists all the importance of tempering (therefore what remains to be said is not really very much). Let us first, as you have remarked, quickly dispose of the chromatic genus relative to the plurality of strings which is now seen in Clavicembali, Organs, and other such instruments, which, I am certain, you will gradually come to confess is not a true plurality of strings, or necessary sounds, but a voluntary increase of them. You will all the more admit, after you have understood, that this chromatic genus is entirely different from Ptolemy's syntonic diatonic, now used for singing and playing.

Gr. Indeed, I have begun to understand about such a diversity of genera. However, continue your argument quickly to its full length.

Al. This genus, or this species of system or constitution, which is formed by the major semitones and by these Diesis — or as they say practically, raised tones, but better called minor semitones — is represented certainly by the epithet Chromatic, which really means nothing else but "colored". From the black colored keys, different

[z] Ch. 14 of Bk. II. Col. 6 of Table of chromatic genus.

from the color of all the others, it is rightly named chromatic. It is the chromatic species according to the distribution which Didymus formerly made of that Tetrachord, as Ptolemy demonstrates in his *Harmonics*[z], and is, in the first place, composed of the semitone called major, contained, as we have said several times, in the proportion *sesquiquindicesima,* that is 16 to 15; then of the semitone called minor, in the proportion (likewise repeated many times by us) of *sesquiventiquatresima,* or 25 to 24; and finally by the semiditone in the proportion *sesquiquinta,* or 6 to 5. This species of Chromatic was chosen voluntarily by the musicians who were our predecessors. They increased the Clavicembalo and Organ by it, because such an increase works out well by providing major thirds and minor ones, and the minor and major sixths, such as there are in Ptolemy's diatonic syntonon. However, with this system one cannot accompany any other chromatic species, nor increase *its* tetrachords in any manner whatever except with *these* tetrachords. And it is truly a marvelous thing that in making such a distribution Didymus did not hesitate to go outside the rules and systems universally held by all the other ancient musicians in forming their Tetrachords in all three musical genera (which system was to arrange the Tetrachord with the smallest intervals at the bottom, the minor ones in the middle, and the major ones at the top — a system Didymus himself observed in his Diatonic and Enharmonic, and also later similarly observed by Ptolemy in arranging the Tetrachord of his syntonic Diatonic), because he placed the semitone *sesquiquindicesimo* as the first low interval, and made of the tone *sesquiottavo* the middle interval, and constituted the upper interval that of the tone *sesquinono,* thus altering the arrangement of the Tetrachord.

And Didymus was truly its first inventor. Ptolemy also gives most excellent reasons for such an alteration in his *Harmonics*[aa], to which Briennio[bb] adds several others. The principal intention, then, of those who first made this broadening was, as we have said, to enable one to have the consonances of the semiditone and of the ditone and of the major hexachord and the minor, as they exist in the syntonic diatonic in their true forms, where, however, they are found naturally — a thing which the ancient musicians did not take into consideration, if indeed, they formed them (the semiditone and ditone), because they did not have any consonant interval either below the Diatessaron,

aa Near the end of Ch. 15 of Bk. I.

bb Near the end of the 3rd and last Ch. of his *Musica.*

as we say, or fourth, until the Unison, or above than the Diapente, or fifth (except however the Diatessaron), until the Diapason, that is the octave. Aristoxenus so affirms in his *Harmonic Elements* [cc], and likewise Ptolemy in his *Harmonics* [dd], and even more clearly Vitruvius in his *Architettura* [ee], in these words (changed into our language) "Neither the third nor the sixth nor seventh tone can make a consonance". I omit Boethius since he was merely a reporter. However, he was an excellent systematizer of the doctrines of these and other leading mathematicians and musical philosophers his predecessors... But you seem to be very thoughtful.

Gr. I am really more admiring, I will say, than thoughtful.

Al. And whence comes your admiration or your thought?

Gr. It arises because having studied many years, as you know, and with many different musicians of the highest repute and among the most excellent of our age, and having discussed musical matters with them an infinite number of times, I have never heard them discourse on these things which fill me with admiration. Therefore I was thinking about asking you if it is necessary for all musicians, such as those of today who compose madrigals and motets, to know these things, and if they do know them, or if simple practice suffices. For it appears to me impossible that knowing them, modern composers would not have made at least some small show of knowledge or have spoken of them as you have now, since in our times men usually like to be esteemed as of more worth than they truly are. But I do not like to interrupt you.

Al. You have made me, ha! ha!, remember a certain one of our modern musicians who, to make himself thought a second Cimabue in music, is always talking with anyone and everyone about "schisma" or "diaschisma", or some other word or musical term, persuading himself that he arouses admiration if not stupor; but who almost induces fear or terror in any listener.

Gr. That is certainly amusing and you are right to laugh about it.

Al. One would believe that he knew much more if he made it his business to have around him books by truly excellent and famous musicians in which are contained important things about music. He has these, but only to examine them and select such words or topics as I have mentioned. As for me, then, I believe it is necessary for every musician to know not only all you have learned from me today,

cc Past the middle of Bk. I & also near the middle of Bk. II.

dd End of Ch. 7, Bk. I.

ee End of Ch. 4 of Bk. V.

but also many, infinitely many, other things and things of greater importance. That the musicians, or more properly the composers of music, of our times know them I wish neither to affirm nor deny. I will say that if they do know them they don't show it, for in their talking and in their writing not the least sign of them appears. Rather they seem to mock and burlesque anyone who is grateful that he knows at least a little. And so what little I know I keep as well hidden as I can and don't talk about it with any one. If today you have caused me to express myself it has been to gratify your desires and answer your questions, and I would have been greatly displeased not to have been able to satisfy you. If, then, simple practice is sufficient to such composers to compose madrigals or motets or other kinds of *cantilene,* I will answer "yes"; since I see and feel that most of them succeed with great applause, and in a short time even youths nowadays do marvelous miracles. But I will add also that it does not seem to me to be a great honor to accomplish things and not be able to give the reasons for them. For this reason, as is said, these composers blush, and their blushing gives sign of their own imperfection. If what I say is not believed, read what, among others, Guido D'Arezzo, the monk, wrote in his *Micrologus,* and before him the Venerable Bede in his *Musica,* and likewise Boethius [ff].

Gr. Now, I understand you, I do indeed. But to understand perfectly I wish to inquire about everything. And to make it come out better and more easily I would like to tell these musicians about our conversation and the discourse you gave me. Thus as soon as they have opened their mouths it will be clear to me in great part whether they do know or don't know about these things. As they say in the proverb, tap the bell and you will know it by its sound.

Al. You may do as you like — but be warned not to meet that fellow of the "*schismi*" right away; for indeed, indeed you could not make certain that he is ignorant either as quickly or as easily as you are now persuaded.

Gr. All right, all right. Whatever may happen, please continue by telling me what remains to be told about this chromatic for I desire to have more pleasure from it. For my greater delectation and comprehension, I beg of you, if it be not too difficult, demonstrate the progression of this chromatic on the Clavicembalo.

Al. The progression of the chromatic, and also the places of the true plurality of strings, I will gladly show you on the keyboard of that Clavicembalo, but I will not be able to enable you to hear the tones, or

ff At the beginning of the prologue of the 3rd book; Chap. 34, lib. 2.

sounds, of the true plurality, as I will be able to make you hear by means of the strings of the Clavicembalo the progression and all other things pertinent to such a chromatic as soon as I have finished telling you the little that remains to tell which is simply that it enjoys all the conveniences that the syntonic diatonic does, and also suffers all the imperfections that the syntonic diatonic does, because of its tempering.

Now look! here is the way it goes. It takes its beginning at that white key which you know to be ♮ mi (where, as I have told you, the diatonic and all the other genera take the beginning of their tetrachords) and proceeding by the major semitone, which is the interval, as you know, to that other white key of C fa ut (I will not pause to recount the ancient greek names in order not to prolong our discussion), to the minor semitone, which is that key, the first of the two blacks, or as they say, raised C fa ut; and from there it takes the leap of the bare (incomposto) semiditone, skipping this white key which is D sol re, to this other white key following — E la mi. And for greater clearness, now that you have seen and heard the procedure of this chromatic in its first tetrachord on the Clavicembalo, I want to show it to you also with pen on this paper (Ex. V). In its

Ex. V. Chromatic tetrachord in practical demonstration

progression it follows ordinarily from semitone to semitone and semiditone in each Tetrachord.

Gr. Since you have done me this kindness unasked, would you please amplify and continue to show me the procedure for the following tetrachord?

Al. Willingly. Such is its procedure in the two disjunct tetrachords, imitating not only in these but in the conjunct, or synemmenon also, those of the diatonic in this manner: (Ex. VI). And these are, as you

Ex. VI. Demonstration of the entire perfect disjunct Chromatic system

may suppose, the four chromatic tetrachords disjoined by the tone of the division, which is the same as the Diatonic and is always common to all the genera and to all their species. Euclid writes at length about it in his *Harmonics* [gg].

[gg] Book 2, Chap. 4. near the end.

Gr. I understand perfectly.

Al. These others now will be the conjunct, or with the synemmenon (Ex. VII) in which the tone of disjunction is divided into two semi-

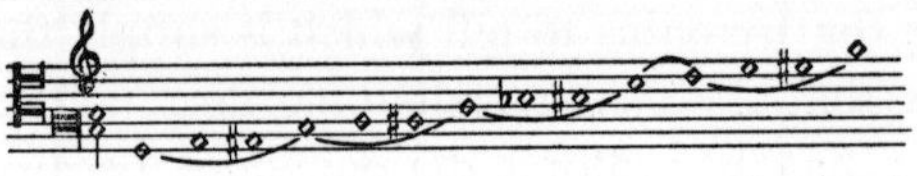

Ex. VII. Demonstration of the conjunct chromatic tetrachords

tones — one major, and the other minor indicated by the ordinary diesis ♯. Whereas the major, which is ordinarily between the disjunct tetrachords, in these conjunct ones becomes of necessity minor in order to follow the rule of semitones and tones, as we have said in speaking of the diatonic tetrachord synemmenon and of *Musica finta.* Therefore the string d la sol re is made less, or lower than ordinary by one of our commas, the which then is added to the following minor tone between the string D la sol re and the string E la mi. Thus, from a minor tone, which it is, it becomes major, and becomes the tone of division a fourth higher in the manner of the diatonic; and about this we have commandment from Ptolemy in his *Harmonics*[hh]. I must also point out to you carefully that in this chromatic genus, as I recall having said another time, the string D sol re is not found, nor is that of G sol re ut; not that they really are not there (since they must be there and truly are) but they are not in the proper places of the diatonic. That of the D sol re is in the C fa ut raised, and that of the G sol re ut is in the raised F fa ut. And this happens because the ancient musicians gave only one name to one string, the same in all the genera and in all the species, Lichanos Hypaton and Lichanos Meson. But the moderns name the D sol re sometimes raised C fa ut and sometimes C fa ut; and the G sol re ut they call now G sol re ut, now raised F fa ut, and now F fa ut. But this D sol re in the place of C fa ut, and this G sol re ut in the place of F fa ut, is properly of the Enharmonic genus. Whoever wishes more particular knowledge about this should read Aristoxenus in his *Harmonic Elements*[ii]. But for our present purpose this has no pertinence.

I will add then that this must be understood true only in the disjunct tetrachord and not in the conjunct. Whereas in the tetrachord synemmenon there is necessarily the string D la sol re, which is the diapason or octave of the d sol re, but less acute than d sol re, disjoined by a comma in Ptolemy's tightly stretched diatonic, as, it

hh Bk. 2, Ch. 4.

ii In the 1st Bk. of his Har. Elem. near the end & in the 2nd Bk. a little past the middle, also in the third.

seems to me, was also mentioned above. The same thing, we will say, happens in *Musica finta,* giving us not only the string of the diatonic D sol re and of the G sol re ut, but also feigning a b-molle in [A] la mi re.

Gr. One can proceed also in this chromatic genus by *Musica finta?*

Al. No doubt about it. But with the same attention that we spoke of in the diatonic.

Gr. Would it be too much trouble to show me also in this *Musica finta* the progression of the chromatic species?

Al. And what trouble or bother would such a small thing as a demonstration cause? Here you are (Ex. VIII). This is in the disjunct tetra-

Ex. VIII. *Musica finta* with flats in disjunct chromatic tetrachords

chord . . . And this is in the conjunct, in which you see the flat (b-molle) on the a la mi re, which Loyset Pieton used in his motet in *Musica finta* "O admirabile"; and the reduction of this to *musica vera* is done in the same way as for the Diatonic.

Gr. One can perhaps proceed with this chromatic genus in that other kind of *musica finta* with the diesis?

Al. Certainly. But you will need some help in the first one, that is, several flats; and in the disjunct tetrachord of this other arrangement. However, in a certain way all the tones appear much better and more distinctly with their simple and proper names than in any other demonstration, because one sees clearly the movement of the tones from line to space and from space to line, as in the Diatonic. Here is the demonstration, and you may see if I speak the truth (Ex. IX).

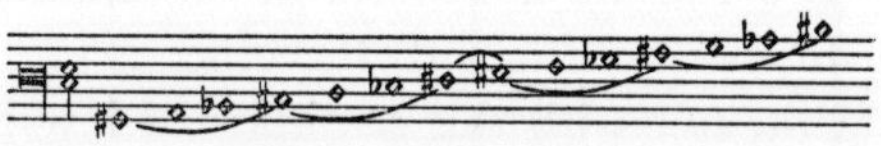

Ex. IX. *Musica finta* with sharps and flats in disjunct chromatic tetrachords different from the first

Gr. So it is; and I believe that its resolution in *musica vera* would have to be made in the same manner, as you said, as is done in the Diatonic.

Al. You believe rightly. Now from this chromatic of Didymus, and from its increase by Ptolemy's syntonic diatonic, you have learned so fast what I was able to tell you briefly about the false plurality of strings that I know you will agree now that it is not a true plurality of strings.

Gr. I confess it freely.

Al. Let us pass then, if you please, to the business of the true plurality of strings.

Gr. Indeed, let us proceed, for I am afraid that I have tired you more than I had intended and than you would have wished. But your conversation is so pleasant and grateful that I would never tire of it, even though you may be tired, as I am sure you are, of discussion.

Al. Now to finish with the aforesaid plurality of strings. To all that we have said I will add only that it would be necessary to add to E la mi another flat lower than its ordinary flat, which was believed to make a true fourth with the ordinary b fa and a true fifth with that other upper ordinary b fa of the synemmenon, for it does not do this otherwise. Therefore it would be necessary, as I have said, to add one beneath the other, which truly would place them in their proportion, for that would lower it in sound by one of our commas. In this way also the ordinary flat of the E la mi would serve to make a true fourth with the added low b fa and true fifth with the added upper b fa of the synemmenon.

Gr. I think I would understand with greater facility what you have reserved to the end (justifying, in my opinion, the proverb "the tail is hard and difficult to skin,") if I could see the description on paper. Because to tell the truth I don't understand it as well as I should like. And what encumbers my mind with difficulty is that I have heard you say that the semitone of low b fa does not form a fourth with that other ordinary lowered (b molle of) E la mi, and the usual lowered E la mi does not make a fifth with the other upper b fa. So it seems to me that just a little while ago, when you said it would be necessary to add another low b fa and another D sol re, you wished to infer that the key of D sol re did not sound in consonance with this of A re to make a fourth, nor a fifth with the other a la mi re, nor a minor third with F fa ut, nor with this semitone of low b fa the ditone, or major third. I did not say anything about these things at that time, in spite of my eagerness to know. And my difficulty comes from the fact that it is a firm universal opinion, held not only by all the practical players of clavicembali and organs, but also by modern composers, who find these thirds, fourths and fifths appear to their ears as they also appear to mine, which, however, I persuade myself are no more perfect and discerning than those of the good Midas — especially after he was, as one reads, adorned by Apollo with that beautiful asinine pair in honorable sign of the good judgment delivered by him in the controversy which took place between Apollo, the lute player, or *Citharedos,* and Pan, the syrinx player.

Al. You have fallen into the difficulty which I hoped to make you fall into; because unless you think about it you would not be able to understand. It remains for you to comprehend division or tempering completely, and with perfect intelligence, as you have shown clearly you desire — but you would not belong to your family if you did not always desire something good. Now I know no other demonstrable description appropriate to clear up your doubt except that of the proportions joined together in sequence, contained in their proper numbers. But I doubt that you have had sufficient practice, as, I seem to recall, you have already indicated in our discussion.

Gr. Could we not try it? And who knows whether you may have made, in such a little time, if not a Doctor at least a good scholar? If you please, and can, show me these proportions.

Al. It pleases me, I wish to, and I can. And, if I am not mistaken, I can write them out, because I believe I have an example handy. Here it is, by my faith! See, under each number there is the character of Guido d'Arezzo which corresponds to it. Now examine it, so that you may get some good from it.

Demonstration of the numbers pertinent to the diatonic tones with additions for true plurality of strings.

			added			added		added		
1920	1728	1620	1600	1536	1440	1296	1280	1215	1200	1152
G.	A.	b.	b.	♮.	C.	D.	D.	b.	b.	E.
1080	960									
F.	G.									

Gr. Indeed, "He who is a donkey and thinks he is a stag will perceive the difference when he jumps over a ditch," says the proverb. I see clearly that it would be a waste of time and, as they say, "pounding water in a mortar," to try to understand something I know nothing about.

Al. I was very much afraid of this, as I said before. However, these things are not easily understood if one has not made rather long study of them and is familiar with them. But if you would like to be able to surmount this difficulty by looking at it in another way, since you have not been able to in this way, with these figures, you can now surmount it with your hearing. I will draw in a moment on this paper a keyboard of a clavicembalo or organ in the proper way, so that it corresponds to the true plurality of strings. Now let us make another attempt, and see if by this road you can satisfy your desire, for the way of the sounds I consider impossible since your ears have never heard any consonances other than those of the Diapason in its true form; and arc accustomed to hear those only as tempered, defective, and altered on all the stable and stable-alterable instruments. And now, as we have no other means of making them heard, I promise you to demonstrate them another time at your pleasure on the Harmonic Rule, called by the moderns the Monochord, that is, an instrument of a single string.

Gr. I accept promptly your most kind offer, and I will avail myself of it whenever I am certain it will not be inconvenient to you. Nor do I wish to conceal my great ignorance in the matter, which I hope by your great kindness to overcome very soon.

Al. If it were not so late I would suggest that we send for the Monochord, but it is really too late. It would not weary you to wait till tomorrow, for then I hope to give you both satisfaction and pleasure. Now I think you clearly recognize that all these white keys are the same as those in this clavicembalo, and they are usually identical in all the other instruments of this species; in addition, some of these semitones may be divided in the middle, or duplicated, one being placed above the other; and because there was a reason for distinction I designed them this way, some all black and the others cross-hatched. (Ex. X).

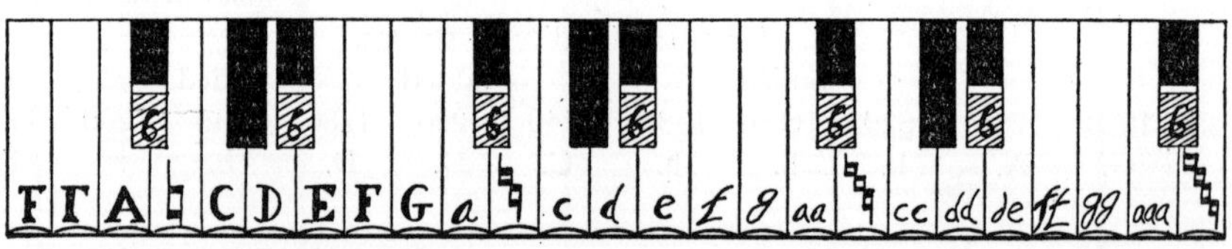

Gr. I see that they are.

Al. Now you should know that all these black semitones have a voice, or better, a sound somewhat higher than their companions the hatched ones. And to give you more clear and precise information, I say that the first hatched semitone of this first pair is the low b fa usual in all such instruments; the other, its companion above, all black, is the added b fa. The next following all black is the added D sol re. This other hatched, then, the first of the second pair, is the added b molle for E la mi. And this second, somewhat higher all black, its neighbor, is the b molle of the E la mi usual in all such instruments. Of the other couple of single semitones, the first hatched is the b fa synemmenon, of which this other hatched is the lower 8ve; and this, its all black companion, is for the octave of the added low b fa; as are all these other semitones — respectively, the acute, more acute, and most acute of all the low ones. Now the function of the added flat before the E la mi would be to make the true fourth, as I told you somewhat abstractly, with the usual low b fa and true fifth with the other usual acute b fa of the synemmenon. And the function of the added all black low b fa would be to make a true fourth with that all black ordinary flat of E la mi. And by its upper added 8ve it makes a true fifth with the same ordinary flat of E la mi. The utility then, as I have told you and affirm under the authority of Fogliano, of the added D sol re is that it makes a true fourth with A re, and a true fifth with a la mi re; and in addition, it makes the true semiditone, or minor third, with the white F fa ut, and the true ditone, or major third, with the usual low b fa. Also, the ditone or major third would be consonant between this added black low b fa and this white D sol re; and the true semiditone, or minor third, would be heard between the black low b fa and this white Gamma Ut. And this, in conclusion, is all that appertains to the true plurality of strings.

Gr. Since you told me that the true plurality of strings is not what one sees in this instrument and in all the other usual clavicembali and organs, which contain for each 8ve 13 strings or pipes, beginning with the lowest white key of F fa ut, I was thinking that you would have to demonstrate that the true plurality of strings means that an octave should contain 18 or 20, or at least 16. But I see on the keyboard which you drew for me and which you told me was almost equal to the false plurality, that the octave is of 13; and among them are numbered two of the usual — this low b fa which is cross-hatched and that black flat of E la mi; when these are subtracted from the true plurality of strings it seems to me that only 11 strings or pipes remain, fewer than the ordinary apparent false plurality by two strings or pipes; therefore again consequently the false plurality is the true, and the true is the false which I hold to be impossible, if not illogical.

Al. The conclusion of your premises would be exactly as you have drawn if one could take these premises as simply as you have proposed. But I must tell you that they are understood in another manner, because the false and apparent plurality of strings is a putting together or an increase of tones, or sounds, of two harmonic genera — that is, diatonic and chromatic together — so that one can serve the other. In this manner nowadays modern practical musicians are accustomed to compose Madrigals, Motets and other *cantilene,* with 3rds and 6ths consonant to several different areas at the same time, by means of tempering. But the true plurality of strings contains only those strings or sounds which belong to a single genus, the genus or rather the species of Ptolemy's syntonic diatonic, which gives naturally and in their true form both ditones and semiditones, both one and the other consonant hexachords. And thus, to 8 strings contained in a

Diapason beginning as you have said, there are added 5, which are more than half of the usual ones. In addition, you must notice that the two strings which you say are (as ordinarily in all clavicembali and organs) no longer of the false plurality of strings for they are of the true, or rather much more proper to the true, in a certain way, than to the false (particularly this black b molle of E la mi) because they derive from the tetrachord synemmenon — if you take away these two from both the pluralities of strings there will remain, both for the true and for the not true, 11 strings or sounds in each of their 8ves taken in your way. So the true is not superseded by the false but remains at least its equal; and, by reason of its simplicity, it will remain the true plurality, and the false will remain false because of its construction.

Gr. I would not have believed that Musicians were so subtle, and could so proceed by syllogisms. But I perceive my error.

Al. You do not err except that you have always esteemed only those musicians who can string notes together, as they say, and who are entirely practical, about which I do not wish to talk further, having said enough. But if you have any commerce with theoretical musicians you will know what they should be; and the writings of the ancients demonstrate it clearly and briefly, apart from the fact that some of them were of the school of Pythagoras, others stem from the Platonic Academy and still others from the Lyceum, or Aristotelian *loggia;* Pythagoras himself and Plato and Aristotle wrote about music most learnedly. And here I protest that neither for this nor for any other thing I have discussed with you today so *al improviso* of music, do you with your ingenuity, nor do others to whom you might tell it, as you have said you wish to do to that friend of the *schismi,* need to syllogize, for I consider myself one of those musicians I have indicated. Such also I would prefer to be, and if for no other reason, then for the authority to be able to stop many abuses in our present-day music, or better, in our present-day musicians. Of these abuses two are outstanding; of which the chief one is the indifference with which they compose the *cantilene,* finding no difference between delightful and lascivious compositions, or between funereal, lugubrious ones and those which ought to serve the divine cult, invoking, thanking and praising the omnipotent majesty of God and His Saints. For this purpose, as Ptolemy exhorts us in his *Harmonics,* expounding the ideas of Pythagoras [jj], was music principally founded. The idea is

jj Music discovered by Pythagoras principally to praise the gods and to excite our souls. End of Ch. 6, Bk. 3.

expressed briefly and with great felicity in the response of Apollo to a lover of the Muses in this hexastich. Listen please, and note the mystery included therein of the hexachord of Guido d'Arezzo that is, of the six ordinary musical notes, ascending and descending.

Candidulo vultu, ruseo, et suffusa pudore
Dic quare in terris Musica carpit iter?
Ap. Ut Repleat Miseros Facili Solamine; Laudes
Sola Vagis Miras Repetat: Utque modis
Divorum: benefacta virum, et pia munera vatum,
De coelo veniens Musica, in orbe viget.

The other abuse would be that of *concerti,* whence began this long conversation. It would perhaps be easy if this conversation should reach their ears, that, persuaded by the many good reasons contained in it, musicians should abstain from *concerti* and not try in the future to make connoisseurs of music laugh at the great confusions of different instruments, by multiplying which they hope to work miracles, such as those they have read about as being accomplished by Orpheus and Amphion and all the other ancient Musicians. And as long as they so deceive themselves you cannot give them good advice.

Gr. You are rising to your feet? Perhaps you have forgotten that there remains for you to tell me of tempering and of those concerts which are so famous today, as you have undertaken to do.

Al. Pardon me — for to confess the truth I was becoming a bit excited and, as the saying is, on my high horse; but this bit of movement has made me wake up and return to normal. I do not wish to fail in anything I have promised you.

Gr. I believed you to be phlegmatic and not choleric. Then sit down again and take up the thread of your reasoning with tempering, of which you should now begin to speak since you conclude that you have spoken sufficiently of the plurality of strings, or as much as is necessary to make me capable of understanding tempering.

Al. If you have understood what the true plurality of strings is, as it appears to me you have, it will be easy, for again you will understand at once what tempering is; for not understanding one you could not comprehend the other in any way whatsoever.

Gr. Your idea of presenting me with this keyboard was truly excellent, for I could compare it with the ordinary one; for that reason I have understood, if not entirely, at least in great part the true plurality of strings which is simple and necessary in order to achieve their perfection and their true form; I can well believe you that this perfection does not exist in the other, or false, plurality of strings, that is, the compound and altered one. I should like to know certain things about this matter, since I don't understand them well, such as the difference between the true consonances and the tempered ones, those called by you defective, imperfect and outside their true form or their corresponding proportions.

Al. About all this I will show you tomorrow on the Harmonic Rule, "Maestro di legno" as it was called by Guido d'Arezzo, or Monochord. For the present it will suffice that you learn that the true thirds, major and minor, the true fourths and fifths, and likewise the true sixths are different from those of this and other clavicembali, organs, and other stable instruments, and stable-alterable ones. You have said you understand and it appears to me that you do know sufficiently well.

So I will go back and tell you that tempering is nothing but avoiding the true plurality of strings by means of a single b fa, and a single D sol re, and two E la mi's to approximate the effect that the two b fa's, the two D sol re's and the three E la mi's would give, deceiving the sense of hearing. I have said "approximately" because it cannot be done perfectly except with the true plurality. And I have said "deceiving the sense of hearing" because one does not have that complete delight one would have on hearing the consonances in their perfect form. But mostly one hears them in this way, either widened or narrowed. The act of narrowing by the master-makers or tuners of such instruments is called "blunting". I spoke also of a single b fa and a single D sol re, and two E la mi's; but you must not understand either one or the other sound, or tone, to be that of the ordinary or the added one, because if you did you would return and encounter the same inconvenience and defect as before. You should understand that it is a sound *between* the ordinary and the added sound which, however, being related to the ordinary keys, can do the work of the one and the other respectively. This is indeed done, as I have said, although imperfectly; nonetheless it is done without displeasing the ear. And such a b fa, or D sol re, or such E la mi's, being only sounds which mark the common limits of each of the consonances, part of which are limited in conformance with their perfection by one of the two b fa's, or of the two D sol re's, or of the three E la mi's, and part by the other, cause each consonance to be increased or decreased beyond its perfection. So then for each act of alteration, which the Maestri call tempering, no consonance departs from its true and proper form farther than the ear can hear and willingly endure, as I have said. So it has been found by experiment that no b fa or D sol re or E la mi taken by itself alone can substitute for these other b fa's, or D sol re's, or E la mi's of the tuners. And this is all that has been written on the subject of tempering; and Fogliano, in his *Musica speculativa* [kk], has written more copiously than any other writer and almost in these same words, except however that about the two or the three E la mi's he does not say anything because he did not know about the second flat of the E la mi. This is remarkable, for he had been a most careful scrutinizer of all the other imperfections of the consonances and a good authority for them. As to this imperfection, information was given by later musicians, and it was aided by the second added b molle. If you wish for me to add my opinion about the origin or invention of the tempering now in style, which Fogliano subsequently describes in the chapter about how practical Maestri attained the one which truly they still use today, I will do it at once to give you complete satisfaction.

Gr. It will indeed be the greatest satisfaction to me to know both things, because in this way it will be much better impressed upon my mind. And if you will tell me also who those writers are who have spoken of it, I will be very grateful, inasmuch as perhaps I will derive pleasure from reading their writings.

Al. The writers who, besides Fogliano, have mentioned tempering in their works, but with great brevity and describing only things pertinent to the accomplishment of it, are these: Don Pietro Aron, in his *Toscanello* [ll]; Gioan Maria Lanfranco, in his *Scintille di musica* [mm], speaking of the way to tune clavicembali and organs; Vincentio Galilei, in his *Dialogo della musica antica e moderna;* Don Gioseppe Zarlino, in his *Institutioni armoniche,* devoting several words to the reason for it, and also in his *Dimostrationi armoniche* [nn]; Don Francesco Salinas in his books on music.

Now my opinion about the origin and rediscovery of tempering is this: that these first maestri, being practical makers of clavicembali and organs, proposed the construction within the limits of the perfect syntonic diatonic system — that is, of the 15 tones, or truly of the 17, including the semitone b fa of the synemmenon and the other of the lower octave — of which this, which I will draw for you, is the simple keyboard (Ex. XI).

kk Last Chap.

ll Last Chap.

mm 4th part.

nn Ch. 41, 42, with the others following part 2; just before the 5th discussion of Ch. 14 to the 27th of Bk. 3.

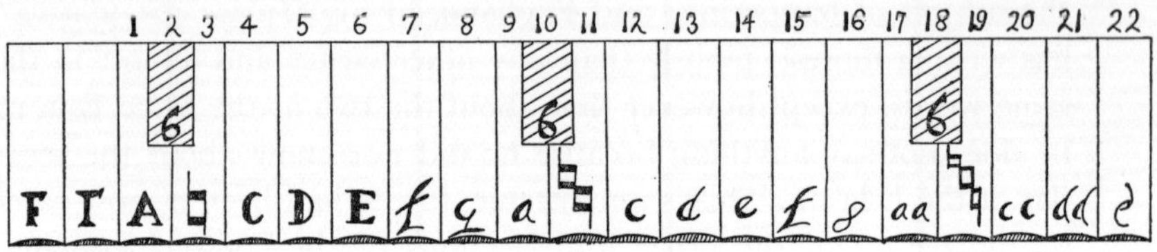

They gave its particular sound to each string or tube, as they do perhaps even today, with the help of the Harmonic Rule or Monochord. When they struck the sounds at the same time to hear the good and expected accord of their consonances, they found not only some 5ths, 4ths, 3rds, and 6ths not consonant but also some of the consonances lacking, or better, considerably distant from their pitch. Knowing also that such a system in itself contains only a certain number of voices, or strings, or keys, they tried to find out if by leaving aside theory and trying the unknown rather than the true proportions of the consonances, they could satisfy and please the sense of hearing, which is the principal object of Harmony. So they fixed first of all, with every possible perfection, the superior octave of the tone (I will speak according to common usage) of this key of C fa ut, the tone judged by them to be the most convenient both in the grave and acute registers, universally called by modern maestri the "tuning note". They then began gropingly now to tighten, now to loosen the other strings of the Clavicembalo, and so to vary the intervening consonances that they obtained a tempered, inbetween sound which, in conformity with harmony, sounded well reciprocally; that is, one note did not approach too close to its perfection, while the other note remained imperfect in such a way that it would be tolerated by the ear, but the imperfection was so equally tempered between them that in their displaced arrangement all of them would be rendered not only supportable but delightful to hear.

Gr. Your opinion of the origin of temperament has much verisimilitude, particularly in view of the fact that all modern tuners daily use, when they tune clavicembali or spinets or organs, regals, and other similar instruments, a system which is very easy for them because of their great skill in their profession, but which appears to the onlooker to be sheer science.

Al. I don't want to conceal my thought about this tempered tuning done by trial and error by such tuners. It is this, that the sense of hearing, (being a sense like all the other four which can easily be by nature less perfect in one case than in another and may even be destroyed by accident) may be less or more perfect, according to the good health or bodily indisposition of a tuner at the time of tuning. If one should cause two different clavicembali or organs — even if they were of the same size and quality — to be tuned by two different maestri (both thought to be careful and excellent) in two different places separated from each other so that they could not hear one another, and if these tunings started from a common first unison for the greatest accuracy of tuning they were capable of, then if these clavicembali or organs so tuned were placed together side by side, I doubt greatly if by touching the corresponding strings, or tubes, one would hear any true unisons except the octave of the first unison agreed upon. Therefore I will say that I believe that it could likewise happen if one maestro tuned the two instruments separately; he would be able to tune only the first unison to agree with the other which had first been tuned by him.

Gr. This seems to me to be important, and though perhaps possible, very difficult to achieve.

Al. And I consider it possible, and most easy, not only because of the supposition I made about the sense of hearing, but because of other material conditions, which for the sake of brevity I don't wish to go into now, which likewise can easily occur in the supposed equality of size and excellence of instruments. And if I thought that you, when you thought further about this easy possibility, would not agree with my opinion, then I would return to get you to reconsider what was said a little while ago in the beginning of our talk about the great difficulty of a group of people tuning together two, three, or a greater number of Viols and other musical instruments. Because of this difficulty is increased the confusion of sounds, which is heard with so much annoyance and causes offence to refined and judicious ears, such as you have shown yours to be.

Gr. You draw water for your mill very well, in my judgment. And now, even though I wanted to hear from you something else about tempering which, if I am not mistaken, you have finished explaining, nonetheless I will be content with what you have showed and told me; and will myself acquire full information of their method from the practical maestri and tuners if, after having read the book which you told me dealt with it, I don't feel entirely satisfied. And so, since you have spoken once more of the concerti — whether by chance or rather, as I believe, intentionally — I wish you would continue, telling me freely your opinion of the marvels, famous everywhere, which our musicians attempt to imitate, not to say emulate and compete with.

Al. I don't remember whether you, when you brought up these famous concerts, almost as proof that there are exceptions, told me the cities in which this excellent art is pursued.

Gr. I don't believe I did.

Al. Are they perhaps the concerts at Venice?

Gr. Are there not others, if I understand well, even more delightful?

Al. And where might they be? Perhaps those of the *Filarmonici* at Verona?

Gr. Those of the *Filarmonici* and those of Ferrara chiefly.

Al. About the ones at Ferrara, meaning principally those of the Serenissimo Signor Duca, I will speak. And because I am able, as their Poet says, to speak of them as a professional, having been several times to hear and see them in public as well as in private, at which time I heard them *in camera,* I feel that the conclusion that I will make about them is valid for all the other similar concerts, excellent and rare and worthy to be remembered and prized. Now listen. His Highness has two large, decorated rooms, called the Musicians' Rooms because there the Musician-servitors ordinarily paid by His Highness go whenever they wish; they (the Musicians) are many — both Italian and Flemish — with good and beautiful voices, and graceful ways of singing, and of the highest excellence in playing as well, some on Cornetti, others on Trombones, Dolzaines, Pipes; still others on the Viols, Ribechini, and still others on Lutes, Citharas, Harps, and Clavicembali. The instruments are placed neatly in those rooms near many other different instruments, some used and some not used.

Gr. How not used? And what are the instruments which are not used?

Al. "Unused instruments" should be understood in two ways; one is, that these instruments, because of their age, are not now employed but are kept because of their shapes different from the ones in which they are usually made today. For example, an Organ in spiral, or screw shape, with the round pipes, of very notable size and measure, made of boxwood all in one piece after the manner of flutes, as many people assert the whole body of the Organ is, and I am not in a position to contradict.

Gr. This must be a beautiful instrument to see.

Al. The other way to understand "unused" is, that the instruments are almost unique because of their rarity — such as a large Clavicembalo, made and invented by Don Nicola Vicentino, with all three harmonic genera and divided into twenty-six diatonic tones with more than 130 strings. It has two keyboards full of semitones, or black keys, double and split. Don Nicola Vicentino is called the "Archmusician" because he renewed the study of the three genera, two of which were almost forgotten, I don't know if I should say by men or only by practical musicians, whereas by theoretical or speculative musicians, of whom there are so few today, they are and always will be remembered. Of the other, the third genera, which these practical musicians always used, they did not know the species.

Gr. Oh yes; this can indeed be called an unique instrument since it contains many strings, not only all the strings ordinarily duplicated but all the three musical genera. It must truly make a strange sound when it is played.

Al. It does indeed. But, as I told you, it is used only rarely because of the great difficulty in the tuning and maintenance of it and also in the playing of it. For there is no skillful master tuner or practical and experienced organist of worth who is not almost terrified at being confronted with such a number of strings, and with the keys separated, as I have said, into two keyboards with the usual black semitones divided in two and others added. Besides, to overcome such difficulties, the player must many times press and hold down with one hand some keys of both keyboards at the same time, and occasionally do this with both hands at once.

Gr. If I said that this instrument when it is played should make a new sound and render new harmonies to the ears, in the touching of the keys it ought to provide a new sight for the eyes.

Al. That is certainly true, both in the one and the other effects: but most particularly in the harmony, when Luzzasco, principal organist of his Highness, touches it delicately in several compositions of music composed by him for this instrument only. But I would not like you to ask me if the division by Don Nicola is then theoretical and reasonable, or is not.

Gr. And why?

Al. Because I rather fear that I would be forced to say no, believing it to have been made thus broadly by Aristoxenian practice rather than by true and good Ptolemaic theory. But let us continue our talk about the order observed by the fine musicians of the Serenissimo of Ferrara in their concerti.

Gr. Yes, please, so that the great desire which you aroused in me by mentioning this Arcicembalo (for thus it appears that the maker himself called it) may be satisfied. I have heard it mentioned on other occasions as being a very rare thing, and truly rare since in addition to this one there exist only two other similar Archiorgans, as he called them. One is in Rome, made to the order of the Cardinal of Ferrara of blessed memory, Uncle of His Highness, benefactor and patron of Don Nicola, and under his care; and another similarly made, but under the supervision of Don Nicola, is in Milan, where its maker died the year following the atrocious plague [1575-76] which not only afflicted that great and opulent city but also Venice, Padua, Mantua, and other important towns of Italy. But continue!

Al. To these rooms then — which I hope you will not expect me to describe in every particular — the Musicians, all or part of them, as they please, may repair and practice both playing and singing. Therefore there are, in addition to musical compositions in manuscript, many, many printed music books, written by all the talented men in the profession, kept in the greatest order in the places provided for them. The instruments are always in order and tuned so that they can be taken and played at any moment; and they are kept thus by capable Maestri who know both how to tune and how to manufacture them most excellently, and who are therefore permanently retained by His Highness, the Serenissimo. Sometimes the Duke, His Highness, commands Fiorino, his M. di cappella and head of all the music (public as well as private, domestic, and *in camera*) to give a *Concerto grande,* for thus it is called, this famous concert to which you refer. It is almost never commanded by His Highness except on occasions when he entertains Cardinals, Dukes, Princes, or other great personages for whom he may be, as he is almost continually, a most splendid and gracious host. And I may truly affirm that there is no other Prince in Italy who offers such an act of courtesy more willingly, liberally, and magnificently.

Fiorino, as soon as he has received the order from the Duke, confers with Luzzasco first if he [L.] had not been present at the command (as almost always is the case from their assiduous and, so to speak, almost constant common service), and then afterwards, with all the other musicians, the aforesaid singers and players; and also he summons every Ferrarese who can sing and play well enough to be judged by Fiorino and Luzzasco good enough to participate in such a concert. With much kindness the Maestro tells them that they must return to the rooms the next day or the day after, according to the length of the foreign Prince's stay. Then they begin the rehearsals in which all these different instruments are used (which you have mentioned and which have been included today in the concert you heard) and perhaps several others also — it does not matter which ones, as I now recall, since I do not wish to divide the choral parts from the instrumental. Then they have not one or two, but a number of rehearsals, during which they maintain the highest obedience and attention, and think of nothing except a good ensemble and the greatest possible union without any other consideration; for that reason each performer comes with gracious modesty when he needs to be instructed and corrected by the M. di cappella. And the Sig. Duca also comes in person, with most kind and serene bearing and brotherly majesty, and when he has heard them often gives them efficacious advice, with his perfect judgment, and admonitions, encouraging them to bear themselves well and to do themselves honor. Then, at the time set by His Highness, they meet to give the concert, to the highest delight and infinite pleasure of the foreign Prince who has come to hear them. All the other persons there follow its harmony with great marvelling, which is truly so great and such that telling about it falls very short of giving its real effect.

Gr. Your conclusion, M. Alemanno, seems to me to be directly opposed and entirely contrary to what you told me of such concerts when we began this discussion.

Al. It is said, things are not always what they seem. Therefore if this, as it seems to you, is not true, it is certainly not very important; because not only do I draw no conclusions from this great concert (though I have explained well, and with clarity, what I have in mind) which might be contrary in any way to what I know I affirmed about the Concerti when we first began to talk, but also I conclude nothing — I simply relate the manner in which judicious musicians act to bring about a great concert, and praise it, not as much as it deserves, but as much as the weak strength of my tongue permits. Now therefore I will make this true and firm conclusion in its honor, which will be (if I do not deceive myself) absolutely in conformity with what I first said about musical concerts — that all of those who try to make similar concerts with so many diverse and various kinds of musical instruments refuse to accept the example of close concord and of unanimity attained by these excellent musicians of Ferrara in their Great Concert. They perform no other compositions than one of two written for this purpose only, one by the late Alfonso della Viola, the other by Luzzasco. There will never be any other composition which brings them to a good accord and which, by giving great delight to judicious and intelligent listeners, causes them to deserve praise. The frequent and so to say continuous conversing, singing and playing together of the singers and instrumentalists work largely to perfect this union and to lessen and minimize the great imperfection of so many kinds of instruments playing at the same time. This is necessary to bring about the sought-after harmony, by which the soul of the listener truly enjoys the hoped-for pleasure and delight.

Gr. If it is true, as is commonly said, that every new thing pleases, how can it be that this great concert giving, as you said, always one of the two compositions composed for this purpose, and perhaps also always played in the same way and with the same persons and instruments, also pleases?

Al. It is true.

Gr. Can it give some, if not great, pleasure and delight to the hearers?

Al. I will give you one reply, perhaps two; and Aristotle will give you two more. My first one is this: if indeed it is said that every new thing pleases, this does not mean that old things cannot also please. My other reply is, that a "new" thing is always one which has not been seen another time, nor understood nor heard previously by the one who sees, understands or hears.

Gr. That is most true.

Al. Then, to these Princes or Cardinals or other such important personages as hear this concert, because they have not heard it before it becomes new; and in consequence it gives to them, as being something new, the greatest pleasure and delight.

Gr. That cannot be denied.

Al. Aristotle's statements, which I read in the *Problems* [oo], in regard to the person who has often heard a concert, are these: we are accustomed to hear with the greater pleasure that *cantilena* which we know rather than the one we do not know, or when the *cantilena* is known to us it appears much better because the end comes out as the hearer expects, so the contemplation is made more sweet; or rather because the hearer feels emotion together with the performer of a well-known *cantilena* — like people who sing a song *sotto voce* and make themselves a companion to the singer — and each one is accustomed to sing with accuracy and grace if he is not by some necessity forced to do otherwise. And to that statement Aristotle adds that well-known music is much sweeter to the ear than unaccustomed. And for this reason, even in our corrupt time, after the singing of a new *cantilena* it is repeated again immediately. So it is with this great concert, the accomplished and judicious musicians repeat the music, whence to them and to the hearers the pleasure and delight is increased, since it is also said that good things often repeated are wont to give the greatest pleasure and delight [pp]. You may take as the final, firm conclusion that nothing is more suitable and more efficacious to produce the expected pleasure and delight, and to diminish and lessen, as I have said, the great imperfections of such concerts

oo Probl. 5 & 41 of sec. 39.

pp Horace, near the end of his Poetica.

than the frequent and harmonious conversation of the singers and players together.

Gr. I believe it, and hold it to be true. For I remember that before seditions and tumults, and finally civil war, began to disturb the most beautiful and fertile land of France, and to burn and consume it (as it has indeed now been burned and consumed); and likewise, before Flanders too eagerly took up arms against its true and legitimate Catholic Prince, and a great part of both countries departed from the true Christian religion and took themselves away from the sacred holy bosom of the Apostolic Roman Church, to vent their feelings, as the good poet says, their bitter spite, with Huguenotry and Calvinism and to become apostate, so to speak, from the most holy Vicar of Jesus Christ on earth — whence came their universal and well-merited ruin — I remember, I say, that from these two provinces and nations sprang, as from two living and overflowing fountains of song, many companies of pilgrims. These people, partly in order to visit the many holy places in Italy, partly from curiosity to see the antiquities and signs of the past as well as the effects of the present splendors of Rome, went on their way lightening their pilgrimage by recalling to mind and singing those graceful *canzoni francesi,* sometimes in three, four, or five parts, with such sonority of voice and so graceful a manner that the people who heard them ran through the streets, lured by the pleasure of listening, and then gladly gave them alms [5]. These people were almost always the first to bring into Italy the most beautiful and best *canzoni* which had then been composed in music by the French and Flemish.

I recall a similar thing to have occurred, with several Paduans who were musicians for important troupes of comedians, such as the *Gianni* and *Cantinelli* and *Donne Sostanze* [6], who represented the persons, clothing, gestures, costumes and foolishness of people on the stage for money throughout Italy. The Paduans provided entertain-

[5] Cf. K. Meyer's *Einleitung* to the facsimile edition p. 19, where she infers from Bottrigari's description of the singing of the pilgrims, the performances of the companies of players, and the singing of the *Rivaruoli* that the music they sang was written in very simple, homophonic style. The exact reading of the text would seem to contradict this presumption as it states explicitly that the pilgrims sang *canzoni francesi* in three, four, or five parts — "the most beautiful and best *canzoni* which had then been composed in music by the French and Flemish". Nor can it be inferred from the description of the *Rivaruoli* that their singing was monodic, or even homophonic in style.

[6] *Giani* are the *Zanni; Cantinelli* and *Donne Sostanze* are names of specific troupes.

ment and *intermezzi* between the acts of the comedy, singing the airs of their Pavanes with the greatest vivacity and ensemble, being all of excellent voice, so that the spectators, even though they had the greatest delight from the comedy, nonetheless were eager for the end of each act in order to hear the pleasant singing. Therefore the wary comedians, conscious — indeed certain — of their popularity sometimes gave rise to occasions in the comedy to sing a serenade under the window of the innamorata, or sometimes at the end of the comedy accompanied public weddings with dancing, playing, and songs.

Al. All that is true, indeed. And even though I have them both fixed in my memory, I did not wish to interrupt your recalling of it by affirming at once that it was true, finding much pleasure in the great enjoyment you showed in your recounting of it. And now, not to interrupt your pleasure but rather to confirm and increase it, I wish to tell you of another similar concert by another gay band in those same times, and even a little earlier. Each member, having attended to his own affairs all day, gathered with the others in the evening; and after rehearsing the singing of certain of their *canzoni* went forth together from the house; and for several hours in the evening, sometimes before supper, sometimes after, and even up till the break of day, went wandering through the city greeting with their delightful songs now one, now another, now still another friend, who were most consoled by it. And their desire to perfect this kind of harmony with perfect union was such that besides seeking many times the useful advice of the Maestro di cappella of the cathedral — a musician of great importance at that time — they never ceased to admonish each other most kindly about their own defects; and finally, standing closely together and, wrapped in their mantles, almost hidden in the darkness, they demonstrated that as they were united almost as closely as they could be with their bodies — of which they would indeed have wished to be able to make one body only — likewise they delighted in making as far as they could a true union of their respective voices, from which then came forth, I will say, an almost celestial harmony. And because they really enjoyed it, and had real honest pride in their work, their listeners heard them gladly, and called their songs *canzoni alla rivaruola* and them themselves Rivaruoli. And it was not without reason that they were thus named because they, not being in a very high position, dwelt almost all of them along the banks of the canal of the Reno, which runs past that part of the city of Bologna which is placed towards the west.

Now to that humble lay congregation which we have just mentioned, it pleases me to add a most noble and high example of the musical concerts into which all sorts and divers kinds of instruments enter in the highest degree of perfection which human and earthly imperfection can achieve. And this will be, I don't want to say sugar on the food, because there are many foods which not only do not require it but abhor it — nor do I intend that our *Ollapodrida* by ill fortune should be one of these — but I will say it in order to close the mouth of our sack full of chestnuts. Now eleven o'clock is striking, which recalls us and warns us to put an end to this long babbling (*cicalamento*) of ours for at this hour even the cicades (*cicale*), having chattered all day, are accustomed to cease their tiresome noise.

Gr. And whatever concert can this be? It must certainly be of a marvelous excellence; and if it isn't the Philharmonic I would never be able to guess.

Al. Indeed, it must be of a stupendous, if not marvelous excellence, as I can affirn, do affirm and confirm that it truly is, because I have had the good fortune not only to have been able to hear it but also to see it being assembled and effectively concerted together, both the first of the many occasions I was shown such a particular favor and on at least one other occasion. It appeared to me that the persons who ordinarily participated in this concert were not human, bodily creatures, but were truly angelic spirits. Nor must you imagine that I refer to the beauty of face and richness of garments and clothing, for you would err greatly, since one sees only the most modest grace and pleasing dress and humble deportment in them.

Gr. You are making me so dizzy with your ambiguous speech, my mind responds to your will; however I should like to see if I could imagine which Concert that might be. But I can't come to any conclusion because if I think of the Philharmonic I feel that they do not fit your words very well for you have used the feminine gender; I cannot apply them to the three most noble ladies of the Duchess Serenissima of Ferrara for her private music [7], since there is no great diversity of instruments, nor great number of them employed in their concerto; they almost always use their most sweet and sonorous voices in singing: — I don't know what to decide.

Al. As you can assure yourself, since I have never heard nor seen the concerts of the Philharmonic Academy, [8] even though I believe because of the great fame of their worth that they might correspond to their academic name, which signifies lovers of harmony, I could not speak of them in any such way, and you may be certain that this

[7] Tarquinia Molza, Lucrezia Bendidio, and Laura Peperara.

[8] Accademia Filarmonica of Verona.

concert is not theirs. Also, I would have had to use words of the masculine gender which, however, even though proffered under the feminine gender nonetheless relate to another, and have in themselves masculine force. Likewise you may be certain that I do not speak of the concert of those three Ladies, rather those three true and living images of the Graces — even though I can testify as to them, because I have been conceded more than once (thanks to the great kindness and generosity of their Serene Highnesses) the grace of both seeing and hearing them. Such concerts are not of that kind, as indeed you have said, in which a great variety of instruments are assembled and about which you have asked me to speak.

Gr. What then may this Concert be?

Al. Don't weary yourself any more, Sig. Gratioso; and if you so distress yourself only because you wish to guess what concert this might be, how you would melt away when you see them convene and play together with so much beauty and grace, and such quietness! You would certainly think you were either dreaming or seeing one of those imagined incantations of the Sorceress Alcina; or perhaps one of those German dolls which by means of tempered steel springs move along the table playing instruments which have been made by their ingenious fabricators.

Gr. Good Lord, what kind of women are these?

Al. — And then finally when you hear the most sweet harmony which resounds in those angelic voices, and those instruments played with such judgment and discretion —

Gr. These are women, indeed?

Al. They are indubitably women; and when you watch them come in (for I will say "come" rather than "go", since I seem to be present there now) to the place where a long table has been prepared, at one end of which is found a large clavicembalo, you would see them enter one by one, quietly bringing their instruments, either stringed or wind. They all enter quietly and approach the table without making the least noise and place themselves in their proper place, and some sit, who must do so in order to use their instruments, and others remain standing. Finally the Maestra of the concert sits down at one end of the table and with a long, slender and well-polished wand (which was placed there ready for her, because I saw it), and when all the other sisters clearly are ready, gives them without noise several signs to begin, and then continues by beating the measure of the time which they must obey in singing and playing. And at this point I am certain you would say, as also in such a moment I say, what the great Mantuan poet says repeatedly in his great poem:

Pandite nunc Elicona Deae Cantusque Movete [qq].

And you would certainly hear such harmony that it would seem to you either that you were carried off to Helicona or that Helicona together with all the chorus of the Muses singing and playing had been transported to that place.

Gr. You told me not to distress myself, and yet you give me the greatest cause. I suffer to know at once where this Helicona may be, and who are these Muses; tell me now, if you don't want me to endure more agonies.

Al. Well then! Ferrara will be Parnassus; Helicona, the holy Church of San Vito; and the sacred Muses the reverend Nuns.

Gr. Then the Nuns of S. Vito in Ferrara make such concerts?

Al. That is the unvarnished truth. And if you had paid attention to the words I said in the beginning of my report, you would have known these women could only have been nuns. And if you should ever speak about this with Wert, Spontone, the Reverend Father Porta, or Merulo of Correggio — musicians properly reputed to be the principal ones of our modern music — and several others who were in Ferrara in the same time I was there, I am most certain that they would tell you the same thing and perhaps even vouch for it more fully.

Gr. It seems strange that I have never before heard of this. But it is perhaps something new, and a work of Fiorino and Luzzasco, since they know how to do it considering their great concerto.

Al. What do you mean, a new thing? It is not at all new. If I were to speak of tens and twenties of years I would not be mistaken. Because of this, in great part, can one understand how the great perfection of their concordance comes about. Niether Fiorino nor Luzzasco, though both are held in great honor by them, nor any other musician or living man, has had any part either in their work or in advising them; and so it is all the more marvelous, even stupendous, to everyone who delights in music.

Gr. That's all right as to the general effect of their concerto. But what about the particulars of their learning to sing, and even more, to play instruments, particularly those of wind, which it is almost impossible to learn without maestri. Being women they cannot easily manipulate Cornetti and Trombones, which are the most difficult of musical instruments.

Al. Those instruments are nearly always used doubled in the music

qq In the 7th book near the end, & in the 10th book almost in the beginning, of the *Aeneid*.

which they play ordinarily on all the Feast days of the year. And they play them with such grace, and with such a nice manner, and such sonorous and just intonation of the notes that even people who are esteemed most excellent in the profession confess that it is incredible to anyone who does not actually see and hear it. And their passage-work is not of the kind that is chopped up, furious, and continuous, such that it spoils and distorts the principal air, which the skillful composer worked ingeniously to give to the *cantilena*; but at times and in certain places there are such light, vivacious embellishments that they enhance the music and give it the greatest spirit.

Gr. I am stupefied; I am truly amazed. But, after all, who instructed them in the beginning? It must be necessary if one wishes to maintain, if not to increase the bright splendor of musical concerts, that there be someone who looks after it, and is intelligent and expert enough to instruct, so that it may be done so carefully and dextrously.

Al. That same nun who is the director of the concerto is also Maestra of all the beginners both in singing and in playing; and with such decorum and gravity of bearing has she always proceeded and continued in this office that her equals, as they are, are glad to acknowledge her and esteem her for their superior, loving and obeying her, fearing and honoring her completely.

Gr. She must have a rare and noble intellect to direct and instruct in the profession of music those other honest and learned persons, especially if they are numerous.

Al. If I remember rightly, there are twenty-three of them now participating in this great concerto, which they perform only at certain times — for most solemn feasts of the Church, or to honor the Princes, their Serene Highnesses, or to gratify some famous professor or noble amateur of music at the intercession of Fiorino or Luzzasco, or by the authority of their superiors; but never extemporaneously nor in haste, nor do they play all compositions, but only, as I said about the great concert of the Duke, those works judged to be prepared.

This as I see and understand, is not what our local musicians do in their concerts. These imitators or apers, if not emulators or rivals, when they try to show themselves most practiced, secure, and excellent, if they don't happen to make any other mistakes, make many errors when they sing. And because of the mixture of a good and bad performance (and now I'm talking through the mouth of Aristotle[rr]) it is inevitable that the concert become much worse,

rr Prob. 44, sec. 19.

finally becoming a real discordance which, because it is so great, often offends not only people of judgment, like yourself, but even the hearing of those who don't have any great knowledge or intelligence of music, who must then leave the hall unsatisfied and almost stunned with noise.

But because of the presumptuous audacity of performers who try to invent *passaggi,* I will not say sometimes, but almost continuously, all trying to move at the same time as if in a passage-making contest, and sometimes showing their own virtuosity so far from the counterpoint of the musical composition they have before them that they become entangled in their dissonances — it is inevitable that an insupportable confusion should occur. This increases so greatly as they continue, that even those (and you see clearly how far this caprice and mania has gone) who play the low part, and the Bass, do not remember — not to say are ignorant of the fact — that it is the base and the foundation upon which the *cantilena* was built. And not standing firm beneath it, as the fabric requires, they go on up, they add nonsensical passages and allow themselves, because they enjoy it, to go so far as not only to pass into the Tenor part but even into that of the Contralto. Even this not sufficing, they go almost to that of the Sopranos, climbing in such a way to the top of the tree that they can't come down without breaking their necks.

Gr. Neapolitan Cavalier, what are you saying?

Al. — Meanwhile the other parts go vacillating, all being in great peril of falling to earth, without hope of having any succor.

Gr. Of all the causes proceeding from the instruments and their players which produce the effect of discordance and confusion, so detestable in our concerts, about which you have told me today, I believe that the most potent and efficacious would be that of *passaggi* unduly repeated without thoughtful consideration. And that explains why I have often heard similar discords and confusions made by the singers in Church when they improvise counterpoint above the *cantus fermus* of the Introit, which because of it often becomes almost odious and ridiculous at the same time.

Al. You may take it for certain that if it is very difficult to do a thing well, even if it is done thoughtfully and carefully, how much easier it is to do it badly if one does it without thought and in haste and, I will add, without any taste, as seems to me to be clearly seen today in all our singers and players. Here is proof of it — they are no sooner in the place where they have to make music than immediately, even if they are late in appearing, they want to rush off to some other place; and while they are singing or playing, they are still able to jabber, laugh, and make jokes with their neighbors. Furthermore, whether the music is sung or played, they have only one kind of expression, so to speak, whether it's a good Madrigal or a Motet; and they are not interested in anything else. And with this I leave you to a good evening.

Gr. This has been a happy outcome, and the fulfillment of my premonition, because it has been just as I truly hoped it would. I beg you warmly, Messer Alemanno, to honor me by remaining to sup with me.

Al. The honor would be mine, Sig. Gratioso. I thank you for it, but cannot.

Gr. Remember, tomorrow you must pay the debt of the Monochord as you contracted with me today.

Al. I will not fail, you may rest assured.

FINIS

VICENZO GIUSTINIANI

DISCORSO SOPRA LA MUSICA

FOREWORD

Vincenzo Giustiniani's *Discorso sopra la musica* was first published in 1878 by Salvatore Bongi, archivist of the *Archivio dello Stato* in Lucca, and was printed in a limited edition of 150 copies to honor the marriage of Cavaliere Luciano Banchi with Giuseppina Brini. It is one of eight treatises found in a codex in the Library of the *Archivio dello Stato*. The codex is entitled *Miscellanea di cose diverse per la Curia Romana ecc . . . Varij discorsi, istruzioni, ecc* . . . and carries the mark O 49 of the collection Orsucci. It had apparently belonged to Nicolao Orsucci, who wrote his name on it and the date 1640. The *Discorso* itself may be dated 1628, or shortly thereafter, because of the reference to Vincenzo Ugolino, who was called to Parma in that year for the marriage of the Duke of Parma with Margarita de' Medici. The contents of the codex are as follows:

1° Dialogo tra Renzo e Aniello napoletano sopra gli usi di Roma e di Napoli.

2° Avvertimento per un Scalco.

3° Istruzione necessaria per Fabbricare.

4° Istruzione per far Viaggi.

5° Discorso sopra la Pittura.

6° Id. sopra la Musica.

7° Id. sopra la Caccia.

8° Istruzione per un Maestro di Casa.

No author's name appears in these essays, but the second treatise is in the form of a letter from Bassanese Passatempo (obviously a *nom de plume*) to a certain Francesco da Domo. From various references to his father and brothers, to his possessions, and to certain events in his life, there can be no doubt that the author is Vincenzo Giustiniani, and it is clear that Giustiniani was making no real attempt to conceal his identity.

The *Discorso sopra la musica* is also written in the form of a letter of instruction to a young nobleman, a not uncommon method of presentation in the 16th and 17th centuries. Indeed, this treatise may really have served that purpose because the language is informal, even colloquial, and the whole tone very far from the academicism which characterizes technical treatises on music of the same period. Vincenzo Giustiniani, Marchese da Bassano, brother of Cardinal Benedetto Giustiniani, was one of the large group of noble *dilettanti* in Rome around 1600 who cultivated *le belle arti.* Of a noble Genoese family, he was a gentleman of culture and devoted himself to the collection of *objets d'art* and other such pleasures. His palaces at Rome and in Bassano, near Viterbo, were filled with priceless art treasures. These he reproduced in his *Galleria Giustiniana,* which was published in 1631 [1]. Living as he did in the shadow of the Barberini and being one of those greatly in favor at the Papal court [2], he had every opportunity to observe minutely the musical life of Rome. Not a professional musician, as he expressly states in his essay, he had nevertheless attained some proficiency in the art and had heard many discussions about music in his own house; he cannot, therefore, be accused of presumptuousness in writing about it.

As a source for information about the period from, roughly, 1570 to 1630 in Italy, the *Discorso* is a valuable document and has been widely used. The opinions and observations of a cultured and noble *dilettante* on music and customs unquestionably present many points of interest to the historian and musicologist, and Giustiniani's candid recounting of the changing styles in music over a period of years provides information not only about various manners of singing and playing but also the names of many of the leading musicians and a catalogue of the instruments currently in use. In the case of a number of the musicians, Giustiniani's reference is the only one we have. Although it is to be regretted that he does not go very deeply into his descriptions of singers and instruments, there can be no question that any addition, however slight, to our meager knowledge of actual practices in performance is of very great value.

Aside from Professor Bongi's limited edition, the *Discorso* has been published only by Angelo Solerti in his *Origini del melodramma* [3], 1903, which is now out of print. The present translation is the first appearance of this treatise in English.

[1] The *Galleria* is a 2-volume collection of engravings by Bloemart and others. Vincenzo's portrait appears therein, with the date 1631.

[2] Vincenzo received extraordinary favors from the Popes Clement VIII, Paolo V and Gregory XV. The Marquisate of Bassano was established in 1605 by decree of Paolo V.

[3] Torino: Fratelli Bocca, 1903.

DISCORSO SOPRA LA MUSICA

Your Lordship has seen already that I remembered to write to you in response to your request concerning the manners and rules to be observed in conversation, to sustain it and make it worth while. Now I am reminded that the study of music may be very much in accordance with Your Lordship's inclination and it seems suitable that I add these few pages to the others I have written, to set down the considerations which have occurred to me *a propos* of this subject, to better satisfy Your Lordship. It is not my desire, however, to enter upon a discourse on the theory of music, which has been taught to us by many ancient and modern writers, together with the other branches of knowledge such as the fine arts and mathematics, in particular by certain authors such as Saint Augustine and Boethius. Nor do I wish to speak of the various parts of music distinguished as canto fermo, figurato, chromatic, and enharmonic, the first three of which are in use today and have been treated by divers authors; of the last we know nothing. Nor do I pretend to write of the origins nor of the inventors of music, nor of those who have perfected it by reducing it to a definite rule and just measure of tones or of sounds in proper proportion, corresponding to the true rules; for I have not acquired such a knowledge of music that I can talk about it with security and without risk of incurring cause for reproof in some maxim or concept, or of being taxed with trying with overweening pretention to enter into *messem alienam*. But because I wish to give pleasure and satisfaction to Your Lordship in the request that you made to me, I will set down familiarly several thoughts that occur to me upon this subject, basing them on the little experience I have acquired while I was conversing in houses where there was no gambling but rather delightful occupations, particularly music, performed without assistance of paid performers by divers gentlemen who took pleasure and delight in it through natural inclination. And to make things easier I will treat this brief discourse almost like a narration in historical form, divided into several different periods in which, during the course of my lifetime, different ways of singing and playing have been invented, brought about by various and distinct circumstances. And in my discourse when it is appropriate, there will be inserted some ideas which, being pertinent to the subject, will not be out of place.

To begin I will tell you that the art of music is placed by liberal men very high, as that art which in order to reach its true perfection should approach, rather than share, the rank held by the sciences. In order that a musical composition succeed in gaining esteem it is necessary that it be composed according to the proper and true rule of this profession and, in addition, with new and difficult restrictions which may not be known to all musicians in general; and not only madrigals and compositions to be sung by several voices, but even the others in counterpoint, and canons, and that which seems more marvellous, the same arias to be sung easily by a single voice. And to succeed in this task the inclination given to many by nature will not be sufficient; there is required also study and application of mind and body. For possessing the rules and the just proportions of numbers, joined with those of the voice or of sound and the knowledge of the effects which are caused by these in the souls of men, not only in general but in particular corresponding to the individual inclinations of everyone and to the taste which prevails in different periods, one may be able to apply skill and experience to his own times, to human inclinations in general, and to the particular tastes of each person. And to attain this ability much application of the intellect is required, and much discussion is necessary to come to some conclusion about the work when the principles have been worked out beforehand. It is not necessary to have studied Aristotle's *Dialectics* and to have learned those verses *Barbara celarent* etc.; but only to unite all the conditions and circumstances above mentioned. And for confirmation of all these things I will say first of all:

1° That in my youth my father (God rest his soul) sent me to the music school, and I observed that the compositions in use were those of Arcadelt, of Orlando Lassus, of Striggio, Cipriano de Rore, and Filippo di Monte, considered to be the best of that time, as indeed they were. And for a solo voice singing with some instrument the taste for the Villanella napoletana prevailed; in imitation of which many were composed in Rome, particularly by a certain Pitio, excellent musician and noble jester.

2° In a short space of time the style of music changed and the compositions of Luca Marenzio and Ruggero Giovanelli appeared with delightful new inventions, either that of singing with several voices or with one voice alone accompanied by some instrument, the excellence of which consisted in a melody new and grateful to the ear, with some easy fugues without extraordinary artifices. At the same time Pellestrina [*sic*], Soriano, Giovanni Maria Nanino composed works suitable to be sung with ease in church, of good and solid counterpoint with good melody and decent ornamentation; so excellent that even today their compositions are preferred to those of the moderns, all of whom obtained from them [the older composers] the discipline which they have attempted to vary more with pretty ornamentation than with basic and fundamental devices.

3° In the Holy Year of 1575, or shortly thereafter, a style of singing appeared which was very different from that preceding. It continued for some years, chiefly in the manner of one voice singing with accompaniment, and was exemplified by Giovanni Andrea napoletano, Signor Giulio Cesare Brancaccio [4], and Alessandro Merlo romano [5]. These all sang bass with a range of 22 notes and with a variety of passage-work new and pleasing to the ear of all. They inspired the composers to write similar works to be sung by several voices in the manner of a single one accompanied by some instruments, in imitation of the above-mentioned and of a certain woman called Femia [5a]. But they achieved grater invention and artifice, which resulted in some Villanellas which were a mixture of Madrigals in florid style and Villanellas. Many books of these by the aforementioned authors and by Orazio Vecchi and others are seen today. But as the Villanellas acquired greater perfection through more artful composition, so also every composer, in order that his compositions should satisfy the general taste, took care to advance in the style of composition for several voices, particularly Giaches Wert in Mantua and Luzzasco in Ferrara. They were the superintendants of all music for those Dukes, who took the greatest delight in the art, especially in having many noble ladies and gentlemen learn to sing and play superbly, so that they spent entire days in some rooms designed especially for this purpose and beautifully decorated with paintings. The ladies of Mantua and Ferrara were highly competent, and vied with each other not only in regard to the timbre and training of their voices but also in the design of exquisite passages delivered at opportune points, but not in excess, (Giovanni Luca [6] of Rome, who served also in Ferrara, usually erred in this respect.) Furthermore, they moderated or increased their voices, loud or soft, heavy or light, according to the demands of the piece they were singing; now slow, breaking off with sometimes a gentle sigh, now singing long passages legato or detached, now groups, now leaps, now with long trills, now with short, and again with sweet running passages sung softly, to which sometimes one heard an echo answer unexpectedly. They accompanied the music and the sentiment with appropriate facial expressions, glances and gestures, with no awkward movements of the mouth or hands or body which might not express the feeling of the song. They made the words clear in such a way that one could hear even the last syllable of every word, which was never interrupted or suppressed by passages and other embellishments. They used many other particular devices which will be known to persons more experienced than I. And under

[4] Famous basso, also the author of a treatise on military tactics.

[5] Famed for his phenomenal voice, Merlo was a violist and composer as well, and a pupil of Willaert and Rore.

[5a] Possibly Eufemia Jozola.

[6] Giovanni Luca Conforto.

these favorable circumstances the abovementioned musicians made every effort to win fame and the favor of the Princes their patrons, who were their principal support.

4° With the example of these Courts and the two Neapolitan basses who sang in the manner described above, in Rome they began to change the style of composition for several voices, both *sopra il libro* and *canto figurato* [7], and also for one or for two voices, at most, with instruments. Prince Gesualdo of Venosa, who played both Lute and Neapolitan Chitarrone excellently, began to compose madrigals full of many artifices and exquisite counterpoint, with difficult, beautiful canonic subjects in each part, all mingled together in such proportion that there were no superfluous notes outside of the fugues [8], the subject always remaining the same even when put *alla rovescia.* And because this refinement of the rules was wont sometimes to make composition hard and difficult, it was necessary to make every effort to choose the subject carefully, for even though there might be difficulties in its composition, the music should be melodious and emerge so sweet and fluent that when sung it would appear to be easy for anyone to compose; yet if one tried it, it would be found difficult and not for every composer. And the Neapolitans Stella [9], Nenna [10], and Scipione of Ritici composed in this manner, following the above-mentioned style of the Prince of Venosa and of Count Alfonso Fontanella [11].

5° At the same time the Cardinal Ferdinand de' Medici, who later became Grand Duke of Tuscany, stimulated both by his own tastes and by the example of the other Princes I have mentioned, hastened to acquire excellent musicians, expecially the famous Vittoria [12], with whom has almost originated the true method of singing for females, inasmuch as she was the wife of Antonio di Santa Fiore, so named because from his youth he was the favorite musician of the Cardinal of Santa Fiore. And with this example many others in Rome practiced this manner of singing, so that it prevailed on all the musicians of the other cities and Princes already spoken

[7] For a discussion of these terms see E. T. Ferand, "Improvised Vocal Counterpoint in the late Renaissance and early Baroque", *Annales Musicologiques,* IV (1956) 129 ff.

[8] Translator's note: As every scholar knows, the exact meaning of many of the technical terms used must be determined from the context. Here the term *fughe* = counterpoint or imitations, but not *fugue* in the sense used generally today. I have sometimes translated this word as imitation, or counterpoint, or canonic subject, according to the sense required. Giustiniani's use of *fuga* accords with V. Lusitano's use of the term in his *Introdutione facilissima et novissima . . . con Regole Generale per far fughe differenti sopra il Canto fermo . . .* Rome, 1553.

[9] Scipione Stella.

[10] Pomponio Nenna.

[11] Count Alfonso Fontanella was a menber of the Bardi group in Florence.

[12] Vittoria Archilei.

of. Then there appeared Giulio Romano [13], Giuseppino, Giovanni Domenico, and Rasi, who learned from Giulio Romano in Florence; and they all sang, whether bass or tenor, with a range consisting of many notes, and with exquisite style and passage-work, and with extraordinary feeling and a particular talent to make the words clearly heard. And besides these were many sopranos, such as Giovanni Luca, Ottavio Durante, Simoncino, Ludovico, who sang in falsetto, and many eunuchs of the Capella; and others such as Onofrio of Pistoia, Mathias from Spain, Giovanni Gironimo of Perugia, and many others that I will omit for the sake of brevity.

The Cardinal Ferdinand de' Medici was then followed by Cardinal Montalto, who took no less pleasure in music, for in addition he played the Cembalo excellently and sang in a sweet and sensitive manner; and he had in his house many professional musicians who were far from mediocre. Among them were the Cavaliere del Leuto and Scipione Dentici del Cembalo, both excellent players and composers; and then also Orazio, a rare performer on the Double Harp; and for singers he had Onofrio Gualfreducci, a eunuch, Ippolita Napoletana, and Melchior Basso, and many others for whom he provided generously. And with the example set by these musicians and all the others I have named, the practice of music revived so that after them many relatives of the Popes, and Cardinals and Princes took pleasure in it. Even all the Maestri di Cappella undertook to instruct certain castrati and boys to sing in florid style and in the new sentimental style. Among these Giovanni Berardino Nanino, Maestro di Cappella in San Luigi [14], and Ruggero Giovannelli developed pupils who had great success; but since these are still living and very numerous I shall not name them now.

6° Since that time there have been many composers such as Claudio Monte Verde [*sic*], Giovanni Berardino Nanino, Felice Anerio and others who, without abandoning the style of composition of Prince Gesualdo of Venosa, have tried to soften and simplify the style and manner of composing, and in particular they have written many works to be sung in the churches, in various styles and inventions for several choirs, even as many as twelve. And this style and manner of writing for a great number of good singers has been continued and is in use even today. I will say furthermore that in our times music has become more noble and illustrious than ever, since King Philip IV of Spain and both his brothers take great pleasure in it and are accustomed frequently to sing and to play Viols together, with a few other musicians to make up the necessary number, among these Filippo Piccinino bolognese, a most excellent performer on the Lute and the Pandora. And further, the King and his brothers write compositions

[13] Giulio Caccini.
[14] San Luigi dei Francesi in Rome.

not only for their own pleasure but also to be sung in the royal chapel and other churches while the divine offices are celebrated. This inclination and pleasure of his Majesty will be the reason why many gentlemen still delight in it, and many others apply themselves to music. As the verse says: *Regis ad exemplum totus componitur orbis* [15].

7° And from what I have just said it may be clearly understood that the style and manner of singing varies from time to time according to the tastes of the Lords and great Princes who take pleasure in it; exactly as it happens in the manner of dress, which continually changes according to the fashion that has been introduced in the courts of the great; as for example in Europe one dresses in the style of France and Spain.

8° Besides these changes in the manner of singing, it may be observed that each nation, each province, almost each city has a way of singing entirely different from the others. And from this comes the old saying: *Galli cantant, Hispani ululant, Germani boant, Itali plorant.* And further, right here in Italy it is recognized that the style and the melody differ from one place to another; as for example the *Romanesca* aria, which is unique and considered to be most beautiful, and is sung by everybody with the greatest delight as something exquisite and most suitable for every sort of embellishment and is accompanied with great facility in every mode; and the same is true of the aria called *Fantinella.* In Sicily there are particular melodies which differ according to the location, for in Palermo it will be one aria, in Messina another, yet another in Catania, and still different in Siracusa. The same is true in the other cities and districts of that kingdom; and also in the other places in Italy, as in Genoa, Milan, Florence, Bergamo, Urbino, Ancona, Foligno and Norcia. I have specified these only as examples, leaving out many others in order to restrict this discourse.

In the general opinion of musicians, in order for a composition of any style or manner to be of worth and pleasing to the hearer, as I have indicated above, it must be written first of all in good counterpoint founded on the correct rules, with novel and difficult passages to weave together in all the parts without burdening it with superfluous notes, sometimes writing it by the rules in the ordinary way, sometimes in inversion.

Secondly, that the entire composition, and the points of imitation particularly, be easy and flowing in such fashion that the artifices do not make them harsh, else they may not be understood except by persons expert in the profession and who give especial attention to such things.

And in the third place, that they be pleasant to hear [16] and have

[15] C. Claudianus, *De IV consulatu Honorii,* vss. 299.

[16] "de buon aria".

unusual grace. I have learned from experience that many compositions by outstanding composers which meet the first two conditions and lack the third have not been acceptable, and remain in the bottom of a chest or on top of a bookcase covered with dust. I could adduce much from this, but being noted for brevity I will say no more. And this third condition is also necessary in the other compositions which are called arias to be sung by one or several voices to instruments; else without it they will be cold and tasteless and, for all their artifice and difficult counterpoint, unknown to others.

From the greater part of the foregoing matter it may be that Your Lordship has a desire and curiosity to know what melody and gracefulness in music and compositions may be, since it causes them to delight and please whomever hears them when they are sung or played. Foreseeing the request that you may make, because I wish to please you, I will say that to answer precisely would be difficult even for someone more learned than I. Nevertheless, without going back to former times as do some people who profess to know something of matters which are very remote, I will tell you what I think is necessary.

In all the professions which require the industry and sagacity of man, *natura naturans o naturata,* as we say, has reserved a part for itself in order to take away from man any occasion to become proud, making him recognize that he is inept and useless by himself without divine aid or favor, making him learn by experience that with all the industry and invention that may exist in any profession whatsoever, it will remain obscure and devoid of glory and fame unless there is added the grace which is a gift of Almighty God, not only in human things and acts but in all creation. As, for example, one will see a most beautiful and decorative woman and she will not have grace, but another will be ugly and will be gracious; a certain cavalier will know the rules of jousting and horsemanship perfectly and yet not possess grace like another who doesn't know so much. It will be said that so-and-so preaches excellently, but lacks grace. One may even say a certain gentleman speaks well and scientifically, but lacks grace; and another who does not know very much is gracious in his speech. One speaks of a gentle and gracious breeze, a graceful horse with a graceful gait. One painter will be clumsy, another graceful in his figures and a sculptor in his statues; and so one could continue with all things created, especially so on earth. But because this is something known to everyone, these examples will suffice. I will conclude with the following comparison: in music, for voice as well as for instruments, one will be able to offer the same reasons for grace and melody saying, by way of definition, that singing with grace is nothing other than a close observance of the style and rules of singing and of those rules for using the voice or playing a good instrument so that it shall not be unpleasant or awkward. It is this grace that customarily brings pleasure and delight to the ears of persons of judgment. And so one can say that a person does not have a good voice but sings with grace as, for example, I will mention again the Cardinal Montalto, who played and sang with much grace and feeling even though his appearance was more martial than apollonian, and who had a scratchy voice [17], as we say. And the same is true of Giulio Romano who, as I have said, was the inventor of a new manner of singing.

And that it is true that grace in singing is a quality provided by nature and not by art (except only in the observation of pleasing modes, as I have said) may be seen from the fact that sometimes a singer appears pleasing to one person and tiresome to another; and on the contrary a stupid singer pleases when he ought not to. And the same effect is seen also in other things, especially in the bordellos of Spain and Africa in which there is not a woman that does not find a market, however ugly she may be. And so it is said also that in the butchershops no meat remains unsold; and the like may be said of other things of which I will not speak for brevity's sake.

I must not omit, however, a marvelous effect that proceeds from music and sound; this has been observed for a long time in Puglia and in the kingdom of Naples with persons who have been bitten by tarantulas, or "burned" as they say in those countries. In this illness which makes them suffer internally so that they must of necessity be continually in motion, almost dancing, they receive great solace and many times total relief from music or sound of instruments; and what is even more amazing, from one particular kind of music or instrument. Among many arias and kinds of music performed for those who are ill, they feel relief from only one sound or one music, as I have said. When these poor people are not cured they are attacked by this torment each year at the season in which they were hurt; and then with different instruments and songs it is possible if not to cure them at least to give them some relief, which is found to be greater than the remedies the doctors give.

On this point I could cite the many and varied effects which ancient authors ascribe to the music used by the Arcadians, and also other fables, narrated as being true, such as those of the sirens, of Amphion, of Marsyas, of Arion, of Apollo, of the Muses and Orpheus, and of still others who were able to move the minds of their listeners to various and divers actions according to the diversity of the style and mode, and particularly with enharmonic music which, as I have said, is not known in the present century. With music they induced tears, laughter, fury, and taking up arms not only against the enemy but in civil wars; and what is more, they made

[17] „voce da scrivere".

the people obey the magistrates and superiors when there was disorder and rebellion. But I will go on without developing this detail, which is superfluous, since one can read what the ancient writers like Pythagoras and Plato have said about it. These philosophers, with others, also believed that there was a continuous harmony of the spheres, proceeding from their infallibly ordered movement, and that all the terrestrial harmonies are similar to this, and with the same proportions, since no other satisfactory reason except experience can be given for the cause of the consonances and dissonances. Notwithstanding the fact that the ancients and moderns tried to attribute them to the proportions of numbers and to the movement of the spheres, this nevertheless does not seem able fully to satisfy the intellect; therefore one is forced to have recourse to experiment alone, and to a *pratique* based on the hearing, not finding any other reason to explain that the 3rd, 5th, 6th and octave are consonances and the 2nd, 4th, and 7th are dissonances. In addition one must have recourse to many other rules of proportion on which counterpoint is based, both as to the duration of the notes and to the different proportions of the tempo, and the diversity of tones and many other things which it is not my business to explain to you.

One could also try to find out the reason why music is so exciting an instrument and one so able to move souls to love, particularly in women; to whom for this reason it is usual to make serenades. But this would be an undertaking rather for an astrologer or a philosopher than for me, and therefore I will leave it to them for the present. Likewise I will leave it to the theologians to explain the devotion and fervor that music arouses in the souls of men during the celebration of the divine offices, and in the uniting of many people's spirits on the occasion of singing together, as may be observed daily in the processions of the religious brotherhoods and societies through the streets of the city. *A propos* of this I will say that a person well known to me chose to frequent a certain congregation, preferring it to many others perhaps better, because its leader and Rector had a beautiful voice when he gave the sermon, and sang the litany well, with grace and with a pleasing tone.

There would remain also to be investigated the reason why, in fishing for swordfish, which one can say is almost hunting, it is reputed necessary to sing, and what is more, to sing with Greek words. Also the reason why instruments or song put human beings to sleep, particularly children and the other animals; and also why song lightens the effort and tiresomeness of the heat for the laborers and farm workers in the summer, even though with singing their thirst increases. And also from what comes the benefit that is commonly believed singing and playing brings to silk-worms, which are called "cavalieri" in Lombardy. And also why singing lessens fear in children while they are walking at night. But we shall leave these thoughts to doctors and to philosophers who know more about them than we.

Songs and appropriate sounds have power to incite the minds of men to various and diverse actions, as I have said, and especially to war; for which purpose are used both the Trumpet and the Drum, at the same time shouting with all the voices together. Thus even the horses are excited and are filled with fervor in the act of fighting; as Virgil says, *Aere ciere viros, Martemque accendere cantu*[18]. And song is a great incentive to drink overmuch, as is done in Germany and also in Italy where they often sing the *berlinghino* [winebibbing-song] for this purpose. I have found myself in Florence in company with more than a hundred persons who, returning from hunting, sang many crazy songs together in order to relieve the tedium of the journey. Among the sailors and porters we see it in the custom of accompanying their united efforts with singing in order to lessen fatigue; and so, too, do those who crush drugs and spices on the Rialto Bridge. Many preachers are heard who in order to move the ignorant and low classes make use more of songs than of ideas, particularly in the sermons for Good Friday. In this way one can say truly that in the effects which proceed from music nature plays a great part, as does skill also; just as it does in the irrational animals and particularly in the birds, to whom have been given all kinds of notes and songs. It almost seems that they compete among themselves to reach a greater perfection and to teach such skill to their young, as being for many reasons necessary to their survival; this is seen by experience, chiefly among the nightingales and parrots. Whence we see that music has a great effect not only on men but also on irrational animals. And if some people do not derive satisfaction from it, as some whom I have known, particularly the last Cardinal Francesco Sforza, that is caused by too great an application of their minds to other emotions which they feel strongly or more keenly. Not being satisfied with one activity alone they willingly shift their attention to anything that presents itself. One could almost say, *nesciunt stare loco.*

In the present course of our age music is not much in use, not being practiced in Rome by gentlemen, nor do they sing together with several voices as in past years, notwithstanding that it would provide the greatest possible opportunity to unify and sustain evening parties. Indeed, music is reduced to an unusual and almost new perfection, being practiced by a great number of good musicians who, trained by the abovementioned excellent maestri, bring the greatest pleasure to whomever hears them by their artistic and sweet song. For having left the old style, which was somewhat unpolished, and also the excessive passage-work with which they embellished it, they now devote their attention for the most part to a recitative style, gracefully embellished with ornaments appropriate to the thought; and from time to time they execute passages with judgment and

[18] *Aeneid,* Book VI, 165.

distinctness and with appropriate and varied consonances to mark the end of each period, in which the composers of today are wont to produce boredom with excessive and too frequent cadences. Above all, they make the words clear, using one note for each syllable; now piano, now forte, now slow, now fast — by the expression of their faces and by their gestures giving meaning to what they are singing, but with moderation and not in excess. They sing with one or at most three voices in concert with suitable instruments, as the Theorbo, or Chitarre, or the Cembalo, or with Organ, according to the circumstances. There has been further introduced into this style in Rome as well as in Naples and Genoa a manner of singing known as *alla spagnola* or *alla italiana* (which is similar but with greater art and embellishment), with newly invented melodies and ornamentation in which the composers excel, as in Rome Giovanni Geronimo, called Il Tedesco della Tiorba. In Naples Gutierrez began [it] and then his son Pietro followed, and Gallo [19] and others; and in Genoa a certain Cicco composes and sings, giving great pleasure to the ladies in *conversazioni* and in the evening parties, which are the custom there more than elsewhere.

This recitative style was usually sung by the ladies in the representations in Rome, as the usage is today also, but it proved to be so crude and without variety of consonances and ornaments that if the ennui that was felt had not been mitigated by the presence of such performers the audience would have left their seats and the room quite empty.

Giulio Romano and Giuseppino, as I have shown already, were the ones who were almost the inventors of this style, or at least gave it good form; and then little by little it became more perfect, to such a point that it seems that little else can be added to it in the future. This style has even been introduced for the singing of Latin verses and hymns and odes of piety and devotion, sung with sweetness and great decorum, and so as to make the words and ideas clear and distinctly heard.

Today in compositions to be sung in church not so much value is given as formerly to the solidity and artistry of the counterpoint as to the great variety and diversity of the embellishments, and to the use of several choirs at solemn feasts with the accompaniment of orchestras of various instruments; even the recitative style is introduced. This music demands great practical knowledge and liveliness of invention and effort to write rather than great maturity and knowledge of refined counterpoint. And from this it may be seen that the maestri di cappella of the principal churches are young men; the oldest among them is Vincenzo Ugolino who is about 40 years old. He was Maestro di cappella in San Pietro for some years and is now in Parma, called there upon the occasion of the marriage of that Most Serene Duke with the Most Serene Margarita de' Medici, sister of the Grand Duke of Tuscany.

[19] Vincenzo Gallo, Sicilian.

In the first and second part of this discourse we have talked of music suitable for the human voice and to be sung; now it remains to say a few things about the various sounds as well as the diversity of instruments. But since it seems to me that Your Lordship may wish to know the difference between voice and sound, leaving aside all that other people have written I will say only that sound, in my opinion, is proper to inanimate things, for it proceeds from air struck or compressed or confined, which is then exhaled and diffused with varying proportions of time and degrees of violence. For example, the property of the anvil and of the bell will be called *sound,* and also that of the Organ and of all the wind instruments and the Viols; and *voice* is proper to all the animals, but principally to man. The usual instruments are Organs, the Lute or Pandora, the Harp, the Cembalo, the Theorbo, Guitar and Lyre; all these are instruments to which one can sing with one or more voices. Then there are the Flutes, the Pifferi, Viols for ensemble and the double Viola or Bastarda, the Violino, the Cornett, the German Piffero, the Sordellino, the Piva, the Colascione and the Sanfornia, and still others that are variations of those mentioned. As, for example, I will say that Alessandro Piccinino of Bologna was the inventor of the Pandora; that is, of a Lute made into a Theorbo by the addition of many strings in the bass and many in the top, and among them some strings of brass and some of silver. It is so constructed that with its range of notes and the quantity of strings it is possible to play every perfect composition exquisitely, with advantage over the other instruments in the trill and in the *piano e forte.* His brother Geronimo (who died in Flanders) played these instruments superbly, and now they are played by Filippo, the third brother, who serves His Catholic Majesty, as I have said.

The Double Harp was discovered almost in our own time in Naples; in Rome it began to be used by a certain Giovanni Battista del Violino, so called because he played this instrument most excellently. And now Horatio Mihi plays this Double Harp almost miraculously, not only in his technic but in his special way of damping the sound of the strings which, if they continued, would cause dissonances and cacophony. Further, he excels all others in a difficult trill. For Organ and Cembalo Geronimo Frescobaldi of Ferrara carries off all the honors, both in his skill and in the agility of his hands. For the Theorbo the above-mentioned Giovanni Geronimo Tedesco, who is also a composer and serves in the palace for private music and public concerts. The Theorbo has been invented in our day and Giovanni Geronimo has much improved the manner of playing it. Then there are many performers on other instruments whom I will not name except the Cavaliere Luigi del Cornetto from Ancona, who played marvelously. Among other performances, he played many times in one of my little rooms to the accompaniment of a Cembalo which was closed up and could scarcely be heard; and he played the Cornett with such moderation and exactitude that it astonished many gentleman present who liked music, because the Cornett did not overshadow the sound of the Cembalo. As for the Viola Bastarda, I have heard a certain Orazio della Viola, who served the Duke of Parma; and lately in Rome an Englishman who played without equal. Formerly the pastime of a concert of Viols or Flutes was much in vogue, but in the end it was discontinued because of the difficulty of keeping the instruments in tune (for not being played frequently they became almost useless), and of getting together the many persons to make up the concert. Then, too, experience has shown that such diversion, with the uniformity of sound and of the consonances, became tiresome rather quickly and was an incentive to sleep rather than to pass the time on a warm afternoon. Playing the Lute was also much practiced in past times; but this instrument has been almost entirely abandoned since the Theorbo has been introduced. It, being more suitable for singing even moderately well and with a poor voice, has been eagerly accepted generally in order to avoid the great amount of labor needed to learn to play the Lute well. At the same time the Spanish Guitar was introduced throughout Italy, especially in Naples. It, together with the Theorbo, appears to have conspired to banish the Lute altogether, and it has almost succeeded; just as the mode of dressing *alla spagnola* in Italy prevails over all the other fashions. The aforesaid Alessandro Piccinino has recently invented an instrument similar to the Plectrum (Lyre?) of Apollo [20], a combination of Theorbo, Lute, Cithara, Harp and Guitar, which performs marvels; but it will not be used much because of the difficulty of learning to play it with the facility with which he himself played.

Playing the Neapolitan Chitarra has been entirely given up in Rome, and almost given up in Naples. Formerly Don Ettore Gesualdo and Fabritio Filomarino played it excellently in concert with the Prince of Venosa whom we have mentioned. The Sordellina was invented in Naples also and introduced in Rome, where it did not continue long since it was an imperfect instrument which pleased only the first time it was heard and then, not having much variety in the consonances and not being useful for singing, soon became tiresome. The sound of the Trumpet is suitable for war and to incite and to direct the cavalry in particular actions; however it is not used by noble persons but by mercenaries. In Flanders because of the wars there are many people who play in a better than average way, and the same is true in England. The same may be said also of the Drum and of the Bagpipes of the Comiti di Galere and of the Germans and the Swiss.

[20] "Plettro" — a singular use of this term which means simply "plectrum" and which here apparently was used by extension to mean Lyre.

Pifferi are used in the armed forces and in seagoing vessels; by those that sail the ocean they are played most exquisitely. They are used also on land, mainly in Spain where they are called *Geremias*; and in Italy they are used in festivals in small towns and country districts, and also in the great cities at the festivals of the common people. This is true also of the bands of Violins. Playing the Piffero or Traverse in the German style, to make musical counterpoint with grace and nicety, is not known by many in Italy. However, at Rome the signor Giulio Cesare of Orvieto was accustomed to play it, and at present it is practiced by a noble gentleman who, among the many virtues and honorable skills that he possesses in abundance, plays also upon this instrument, to the amazement of those who hear him.

The playing of the Sanfornia, which in Rome is called by a foul name and in Lombardy Viabò, is not worthy of being brought up, as it is seen ordinarily in the mouths of the rabble. But having been ennobled by Signor Ottaviano Vestrij, who plays it with a musical intention and with accuracy in the intonation of the notes, I shall not omit it; many times I have heard him play, among other madrigals, that of Luca Marenzio which begins *Vestiva i colli,* etc. In Antwerp I have heard the same madrigal played on the bells in the campanile of the principal church. The player had the book before him and touched the keys, as one does with Organs; and he himself told me that this was the custom in Bolduch and in other places of Brabant and Flanders. A certain Francesco Tunnilla, a goldsmith in Bologna and a man widely esteemed, has invented a brass ball which encloses some machinery inside it; at the least motion it sounds an unexpected harmony, to the delight and marvel of the hearer.

This narration will seem long and tiresome to Your Lordship, especially with the names of so many persons. But if you will have consideration for my intention to give you ample satisfaction, and to the kind of material which it treats, you will readily recognize that I would have written badly in another manner in attempting to explain the different kinds of music and the changes which have occurred at distinct intervals of time according to the circumstances. These have aroused many fine talents to find new inventions to present for everyone's pleasure, and to profit themselves from it, as at present there are many people who, with the profession of music, have earned more than a thousand *scudi* of income; one cannot begin to name them all. However, this is not a discourse on political theory composed, or to say better, stolen from good writers both ancient and modern as is the practice of many writers today, but it is a true account in the guise of telling of facts and relating history based on what little knowledge I have acquired, as I said, during the conversations engaged in by many lords and gentlemen in my house where, among other honorable practices, making music was the custom.

INDEX OF AUTHORS AND WORKS CITED IN *IL DESIDERIO*

INDEX OF NAMES

INDEX OF SUBJECTS